The
Throbbing Moon
and the
Three Season Tango

A   M E M O I R

Michele Wheeler

Distributed by Bublish, Inc.

Paperback ISBN: 978-1-64704-152-6
eBook ISBN: 978-1-64704-153-3

*To Jon,
Lily and Caitlin*

Table of Contents

Prologue

I left Jon alone to read it and could think of nothing else until he was done. This wasn't the first piece my husband had read. For nearly a year, I'd been capturing random moments in what I was starting to think were chapters. It started with those small moments of clarity, some resolution about how my inherent change in perspective was to be applied in this new life. I needed to hold on to those moments, to anchor myself securely to anything I could recognize as the me I'd known so well for 43 years. *Yes! That's it! That's who I want to be as I'm living with cancer.*

It's not that I haven't spent much time writing. It's been a constant throughout my twenty-year career in water science: technical writing that reports data sans emotion, leisure pieces that make the technical approachable for non-scientists, and ethos-driven proposals to grab the attention of funders. But not one of those writings held the pronoun "I." They removed personality or instead assumed an organizational one. But in this writing, "I" was at the heart of it all.

I didn't start writing after my first diagnosis, a relatively friendly stage two breast cancer. It was treatable, in a way I'd likely beat, yet still terrifying none the less. It changed me, without question. I was still passionate about caring for rivers and lakes. My work to bring people together to protect and restore them still fed more than it asked of me. But I didn't even consider working the 60-hour weeks that were the norm before cancer. Jon and my twin daughters, Lily and Caitlin, were only nine back then. They always held the center space in my world, but that space got bigger, and I turned to it far more. There was a shift in nearly every facet of my life that came without deliberation, without question, and was absolute.

But the need to write from the heart didn't start until my cancer returned with a stage four tag nearly five years later. I wrote to slow down, to focus my attention in healthy places, to glue myself back together. Jon was beside me the whole time, always my greatest place of comfort. Yet as I captured our past and present with words on paper, we both came to see a deeper view of our shared history, and in each other. That I was writing was new and some insights into the life we'd been living together so tightly were new. But what Jon was reading now was different from everything else so far. Still my story but told in a voice neither of us knew was there.

When it seemed like I might actually be doing this - writing a memoir - I started searching for what to call the thing. By then I was hundreds of pages in but couldn't find the few words for the perfect title. There was a hefty pile of well-placed title rejects.

One morning, Jon and I laid in bed in the early space between sleeping and waking. The girls, now 14, weren't yet awake either.

So, I nestled my head on Jon's shoulder as he wrapped me up and rested in the steady rise and fall of his breathing. After a few moments of listening to the quiet of our home, Jon said quietly, "I dreamt the title of your book last night."

I grinned into him, "Oh yea?"

"Yep. You told me it was 'The Throbbing Moon and the Three Season Tango.'"

I opened my eyes. "What?" I laughed. "Any chance I told you what that means?" Jon shook his head with a grin and fell back asleep.

Over the next few days I could not stop thinking about the title. The more the moon, the seasons and tango rolled around in me, the more I realized how perfectly they fit. It was as if Jon had absorbed the core of my story, his subconscious able to process what all my intentional effort could not. It was the emotional story of my cancering, one best told in a foreign world.

Jon was upstairs reading the first chapter in that world. I feigned tidying up the house as an excuse to pace while he read my latest chapter. He must have read it at least twice because I got a lot of tidying done.

When he finally came downstairs, he found me sweeping the kitchen, and I summoned all my self-control not to accost him with questions for affirmation.

He sat down slowly at our kitchen table, looking confused and cautious. Then he looked up at me with those wrinkles between his eyes that tell me he's fulling considering something and asked, "Who are you?"

I let the broom fall and rushed to hug him hard, pulling away to hold his shoulders and exclaim, "Exactly honey! Exactly!"

Spring

The echo is ruthless. The beat of every step bounces off the cement walls, following her up the stairwell. She is the one with these shiny black shoes, the pumps with the sturdy heel. She is the one, with each step, creating a tidy rap that reverberates back over itself and collides with all her other tidy raps. The compilation of all those steps - twenty floors worth - are pounding through her head like something from the fringes of out-there acid jazz. *This can't be right,* she thinks, staring straight down. *Can it?* At the next landing, she looks up to see how much further she has to go, but there is no end in sight. She's miscounted the number of flights. She puts her head back down to keep moving in a steady slog of a pace.

At least ten stories later, she reaches the top of the stairwell. The lack of introduction still surprises her: such a simple metal door. When the palm of her hand feels the cold of the door, she pauses. *Wonder what I'm dancing with tonight?*

She braces herself for the screech of grating metal on metal as she pushes into the door. Every time she slips through this entry, she feels like she's breaching an invisible barrier. Like she's walking through a membrane that separates them from the rest of the city. A faint murmur of the outside world still penetrates though. She can hear the traffic on 5th Avenue competing with the waves breaking on the beach just a few blocks away. A sliver of the shore is just barely visible between the buildings in front of her. This early in the season and this late at night, only the riffraff will be there, lining the shore in pockets of raucous good fun. She can't see any of them from the roof, but she knows they are there.

She knows because she used to be one of the partiers on the beach. Last year at this time, she'd probably be on her way there by now. She liked it better when winter's chill still clung to the night. It kept the beaches clear of the meek. She'd drag a cooler out there with her crew, far away from the crowds downtown. They'd always end up with a few more revelers hanging around than they started with on those nights. Life was so easy, talking about nothing and laughing until the sky lightened at dawn. It was the absence of heavy thoughts that strikes her now. How wonderfully frivolous life was then.

It's nearly dark out; the twilight offers just enough light to see him sitting in the lone metal lawn chair on the roof. He always gets here early, just sitting on that cold hard chair and staring at the asphalt under his feet. She can tell that the door startled him by the awkward way he turns around to give her privacy, and she is thankful that she won't have to say anything or look at him even.

She walks in front of him and heads directly to the far side of the roof. Theirs is the tallest building in the city. The only other building that even comes close stands just a block over. She watches it. Waiting. Until the glow begins to hum from atop it and the moon emerges, without charge or caution. Just a perfectly smooth ball of rock. She stares it down with her back to him, her arms folded across her chest to keep warm. Just then, it strikes her as odd that the moon can float in the sky. It shouldn't be possible for the moon to rest suspended there, to be so persistent. On cue, the moon throbs brighter. The shine of its pulsing makes it seem to expand. She stares at it harder. Is it getting bigger? Or is it just the glow? She feels his presence behind her, feels that he has seen it too. He's wondering.

She turns around to see him standing in front of his chair, mesmerized by the moon. He is leaning into it with both fascination and horror. She waits to let him take it in. He is still fixated, so she steps toward him to catch his attention, to coax him back here. It's only when she's nearly beside him that he startles back to the present. He tries to hide his trance. But his eyes are so wide, the slim smile so forced, his energy is palpable. He is completely overwhelmed.

As he sits back down to put on those shiny black shoes, she realizes she has no idea how that chair got here. It's just another fixture, another object that has become absurdly familiar. She watches him study his shoe, turning it over to look at the smooth sole. He holds it lazily in front of him, taking in the shape of it. He scowls, *Why pick shoes for dancing that are so hard on the feet?* She stifles a sigh of annoyance, and he sighs lightly himself, more an extended exhale, as he reaches down to take off one of his worn, ratty sneakers.

She thinks back to the days when the moon would wax and wane. Sometimes it would even take a rest, allowing all the stars to coat the night. She looks back towards the shoreline and remembers so clearly a night with a gibbous moon perched willingly above the beach. The nights before Tango took command. But now the moon has been full for weeks.

He clears his throat, interrupting her thoughts of the moon, pulling her to Tango.

They've been learning the dance. It is fully prescribed. They know the moves. They just need to execute them. An accordion whines an intro, and a violin lays down a bittersweet melody over it. They each hesitate, neither confident enough to take the lead. It's not their first Tango, but they are far from comfortable here and excessively polite to cover their unease. He grimaces uncertainty. She smiles softly, stands a little taller, and guides his hand to her waist, feeling him relax when she sets it there. She takes a step forward. He matches it with a perfectly timed step backwards, and they begin.

They both had seen the fresh head flips and across the room strut of Hollywood Tango, a dance about lights and cameras. But they need no light here. The moon is now shocking. It's not the size but the brightness that hovers so close it threatens to swallow them. After weeks of the full moon's consumption, she is annoyed that it continues to steal the night. *We are dancing here! Let us dance!*

It is a repetitive dance, Tango, and they put in their time at the edge of its mayhem. They dance with broad dramatic strides, occasionally tripping over each other. But they manage. They keep at it, trying to find balance in the chaos.

And on it goes. The Tango in response to the relentless force of the moon. They never forget the moon. Its gravity pulls without conscience. The sky is their audience, captivated by the lone dancer on the roof. Just one. They are different moods around the same moment, two halves of a singular whole. Whether or not they are good at Tango is irrelevant. They only hope its work will be enough.

This is happening

I walked through the forty-acre grove of maples that we tapped for maple syrup in the spring. It was more open here because the trees were bigger, the canopy so dense it shaded out the understory. I stopped to look up at the small valley of our property, the stems of big, old maples standing strong around me. This spring, just six months ago, there were hundreds of buckets hanging from all these maples catching the drip... drip... drip... of maple sap, thin as water. Our eight-year-old twin daughters, Lily and Caitlin, would run from tree to tree, eager to see how much each bucket had filled up overnight. We all knew the ones that filled well, the others that were usually slim. When I'd pick up the bucket to empty it, the girls would stand on their tip toes and open their mouths wide to catch a few drops straight from the tap. They were joy and light, the epitome of in-the-moment, taking in the beauty around them.

I was not in the moment. I didn't know where I was.

I kept walking, thinking about the way he said it. Not concern, that would imply some emotion, some investment in the answer. "You need to get that biopsied," completely monotone, staring straight at the floor, hands loosely clasped behind his back, and trudged around the table I was lying on. "You'll need a referral," he said as an afterthought as he walked out of the exam room.

That was just hours ago. That's what I kept seeing, kept replaying over and over as I walked around our trails on a Friday afternoon. Jon put these trails in shortly after we built the place about eight years ago. I stared straight down as I walked, head down like the ultrasound doctor, but with completely different intention. I was trying to walk off panic, trying to match panic's intensity with the speed of my walking. There was no shortage of emotion here. I was *fully* invested in the answer.

I thought back to the times when the girls would stay inside during sap collecting, our house settled in the middle of our woods, an island of trees surrounded by hay fields. With just Jon and I emptying buckets, those times were more quiet. I'd stop for a moment in the middle of the maple grove, listening to the different tones of sap hitting buckets of varied fullness. A gentle pinging from all around me - some near, some far - ethereal, like a random assortment of xylophone notes, but in perfect harmony. The peace of that seemed forever ago, if it ever existed at all.

I kept walking, re-examining the ultrasound doctor's intonation, his movement, trying to interpret meaning in it, if there was an absolute answer in it. It seemed like there was. As soon as he left the room, I asked the ultrasound tech, "What in the hell just happened?" The look on her face told me she knew exactly what just happened. But since a technician can't offer interpretation, she fumbled through some non-committal explanation of the kinds of things one might look at, when one is evaluating such imagery. It was awkward for both of us.

As soon as I left the exam room, I called my primary care doctor, Kathy, frantic for a referral. Kathy was my doctor, but also a casual friend. She said, "Get back in there," and called in the referral right away. So back in I went to face the ultrasound doctor for the biopsy right then and there. I kind of hated him at that point, which might not have been fair. I ignored him as much as he ignored me and toughed out the biopsy of my breast, astounded by the size of the needle he rammed into me, unable to believe that this was happening. I walked out of there with a numb breast and an equally numb mind and called Jon as soon as I reached my car, fear making me talk so fast, scattering my words into a non-linear rambling. Jon was steady as ever. "Let's wait and see what they say on Monday." He held that line all weekend. Entirely reasonable. I found it enormously unsatisfying.

At 37, I had no personal experience with cancer. Instead, images from all the movies I'd seen would flash in disconnected bursts. Would I lose my hair? Would I be horribly sick during treatments? Would I... But more so, I started thinking about the more immediate implications of a possible cancer diagnosis. We had been planning to sell our country home for the convenience of in-town living with kids. Our house had been on the market for years with very few perspective buyers. The plan was to move 40 minutes north into the small town of Washburn, nestled on the coast of Lake Superior in northern Wisconsin, which would mean the girls would change schools. Can you make a move while undergoing cancer treatment? What would our insurance really cover? How do I continue to exist with this happening?

How would I tell the rest of my family?

That's what got me. But I pushed it down and kept walking. Yesterday, there was none of this. Life was completely normal. I physically felt perfectly fine. I still felt perfectly fine, but it was starting to look like I wasn't perfectly fine.

I came to a small opening in our woods, a spot lined with soft grass. I saw the four of us there at a picnic earlier this summer, batting away mosquitoes, chomping sandwiches and rolling around in the soft grass like freedom. I wondered now if cancer had been growing then, wondered how unaware we all were.

Back at our house, I focused all my attention on the girls for the weekend, bursting with gratitude for their light banter, for the distraction to help me pretend this wasn't happening. They bounced around our living room with their pig tails and freckles and the excitement of third graders. They showed me their school papers. We drew pictures in the evenings. But under the normalcy, I ran a non-stop narrative to prepare myself for whatever news I'd receive, having no idea what it meant to be "prepared."

The reality became even more palpable as soon as met with Kathy the next Monday. Most of my appointments with her were regular check-ups or minor ailments with ready fixes. Mostly we'd laugh at how adorable my girls were as toddlers. But that day, she fidgeted, stalled by picking up the pathology report and putting it back down again. So different from the Kathy I knew at our house for dinner when the girls were just 1-year-old. She would hide a ball under one of three cups, and they'd study her intently as she slowly mixed them up. Caitlin, always more eager, would charge right in and grab the cup, then shake it with utter joy when she uncovered the ball. She'd shriek with triumph and throw the cup across the room. Kathy laughed along; Caitlin's energy was absolutely contagious. Lily, more hesitant, would study the moving the cups, tracking the hidden ball, but also searching for Kathy's intentions on this round, how they might change on the next one. Lily would look stoically at Kathy and calmly grab the cup with an expression that said *again.*

I had never seen an uncertain Kathy, one that was reluctant. She scanned the room as if looking for the words to say next. It slightly settled me, actually, to see someone looking as overwhelmed and distraught as I felt over the past few days.

She took a deep breath before turning to look directly at me, "The pathology came back as a mucinous carcinoma." By then I knew. It was almost a relief to put a name to it. I focused intently as she rushed through the details. "It's a rare kind of breast cancer. A more gelatinous form that is often misdiagnosed because it doesn't feel like other cancers." *Ah ha*, I thought. *That's why they called that spot just thickened breast tissue two years ago.* "Usually much older women get this kind of breast cancer. It tends to be slow-growing, tends not to invade to other parts of the body, and is considered very treatable."

I was taking it in. Slow-growing sounded good. Tending not to invade sounded good. Compared to what I had imagined over the weekend, this was fantastic. Although still cautious, I felt a little weight lift. Kathy talked through our next steps, namely, getting rid of the lump. Our hospital in Ashland handled the small stuff. For the big stuff, locals from our area drove to the hospital in Duluth, an hour and a half west of us. This was big stuff. Kathy left to get my follow-up appointments rolling in Duluth.

I turned to Jon for the first time since entering the room. He half-grinned, half-grimaced and put his arm around me. As

I nestled into him, I felt the tension of the weekend melt away ever so slightly. We could deal with this. It was a friendly cancer. We'd just take it out and it would all be okay.

Jon and I called our neighbors and asked them to watch the girls after school so that we could make some sense out of all this over dinner. We talked over every word Kathy said, repeating them in part to believe them. There were big pictures choices to make, but the more immediate decision was whether or not I should go to a town board meeting that evening. I was the Director of the Bad River Watershed Association, a small environmental non-profit. I'm talking really small. We had just grown from a staff of one (me) to three in the last year. I was on the agenda to present, and the meeting with the town leaders started in little over an hour. They were interested in making sure cars could get over streams, and I was interested in making sure fish could get through the culverts under the roads. My job was to build relationships with these people, convince them of our competence so that they'd be open to having road management include care taking of streams. I had data to share on the pipes that didn't let fish swim through them, the ones to replace. Last week, this was important. Last week, I loved taking the complex science of streams and fisheries and making it something non-scientists would care about. I loved bringing people who may not think of themselves as environmentalists into the conversation. But now, I didn't even know how I'd talk about something so trivial.

But I didn't skip meetings. All weekend, I had been obsessing about how a cancer diagnosis would change things for me, but now it was known, it was treatable, and I was ready to move on. I wanted to be a director—not a whimpering, scared cancer patient. Enough of that.

Jon was more hesitant about moving on so quickly. He convinced me to cancel, out of a presumed lack of effectiveness. *You're sick and you can't go* didn't resonate, but *If you postpone, you'll really be able to bring your A game* did. I considered this and figured a cancer diagnosis was a pretty solid reason for a night off. "But what do I... tell them?"

Just hours into my cancer diagnosis, I was forced into the intensely uncomfortable position of all cancer patients: Who do I let in? And how far? Jon and I watched each other, imagining how each scenario could play out, and the implications of different approaches. *Maybe I'll just skip it and not even call* was quickly dismissed. No integrity there. A vague, non-answer for a last-minute cancel—*something came up*—would certainly give the impression that I was a flake. So how about just throwing it out there? When I'd test it out in a mock call, simply saying the word "cancer" would tie me up into silence. It felt far too intimate for these near strangers, when I couldn't even believe the words yet myself. Jon just listened, nodding with how incredibly awkward it was. Even though Jon was with me, the decision on how to navigate this was mine alone. I've always hated people telling me what to do, but right now, with so much to take in at once, it would be nice if someone could take the decision-making burden from me. And since I'm ordering up fairy tales, let's just go ahead and make it an all knowing, enlightened, perfect and *easy* decision.

I decided to let people in; I didn't know how to be any other way. Because I love people, and in particular, the sincerity of our relationships with one another. I value the honesty in people sharing their truths. They invite connections that help us to better understand each other. I couldn't imagine acting out one life while pretending my new reality didn't exist. I started making a series of phone calls in which I said "I have cancer" over and over.

This was really happening.

Re-arranged

T his was actually happening, and it was going to demand some changes around here. Some of the changes that cancer brings are sharp and immediate. But I'm a problem solver. Always have been. I'd figure them out. It's a trait I've learned and inherited largely from my mom. When I was in high school in the suburbs north of Pittsburgh, my mom and I would sit for hours at the dining room table working though my calculus problems. Our interest would build with every transformation and equation. We even enjoyed the frustrations of getting it wrong and having to circle back, because it made figuring out something hard all the sweeter. Until finally, a multi-paged scramble of letters, symbols and numbers would emerge in solution. One that made perfect sense. We'd sit back and grin at each other. How enormously satisfying.

I didn't know the rules or building blocks for cancer though. I didn't know the language. When I tried to assemble my new reality, tried to think my way through a next logical step, my mind was mostly blank. A complete inability to see any part of how to think through this. It was a completely foreign feeling.

I started with creating a way to keep friends and family around me updated. Even just days in, I could see that the repetition around repeating my status was suffocating, a relentless reminder of how much it all sucked. My sister, Heather, stepped up to help. Which was a big deal. We were close growing up and into our thirties, but tensions that led to an argument—one that could only be covered in a separate book—drove a solid stubborn wedge between us. Before my diagnosis we hadn't spoken in over a year. Cancer is kind of handy in that it scrapes all the bullshit away and leaves what's really important. I loved Heather. A lot. She loved me. A lot. I spent a lifetime as her little sister and needed that. When she called, we skipped the reconciliation talk entirely and just started planning out an invite only website to let the people around me know what was happening.

For my first post. I figured I'd give the cliff note version of the questions that came up most often. I focused more on framing how I wanted to talk about cancer. Before cancer, I saw people at the grocery store and shared brief, witty banter on my way to pick up a pizza for dinner. After cancer, I would get hung up in nearly every aisle. *What's happening? How* are *you?* The solemn talks with sympathetic, furrowed brows just dragged me down and made me not want to leave the house. I was really just trying to pick up a pizza.

I led people into the way I wanted to deal with cancer by letting everyone know that we can still be us, despite cancer.

Posted by Michele Wheeler, October 14, 2011

> *... after talking with the Doc for a while about the type of cancer I have and how treatable it is—there is a 97% survival rate after 15 years with mucinous cancer, 97%!!!—I felt GREAT!! I told Jon when we left the appointment that I'm THRILLED to have mucinous carcinoma. Best breast cancer to have. The word mucinous, before the word carcinoma, is a reason to celebrate.*

It was a fairly easy post to write because in contrast to what I had been imagining, I thought I'd make it through just fine. I didn't dread leaving the house as much after that and found my smile again when I saw people. It made me feel like we were all in this together, which was an enormous comfort.

Figuring out how to manage work and cancer was more complicated. My work consumed me. Because it wasn't just a job, it was an expression of my values. My love of water started with my grandfather: Grandpap. He had a special kind of light about him. Just being around him, you couldn't help but absorb the beauty he saw in the world, and in people. It was in the way he'd brighten when I'd tell him about anything I did. The way he'd look with sincere amazement at a stick figure drawing I drew for him when I was little. He'd see immense potential, and brag that I was a "down right art-teest!" I was not a talented artist. But he believed so much in me that I believed in myself.

When I was a kid and through high school, he'd take me fishing at his trailer camp a couple hours north of Pittsburgh. We'd putter around the lake in his little aluminum boat to all his prized fishing spots while he recounted his best catches over the thirty years he'd fished every inch of that water. I soaked up every word. He'd set up my rod and talk me through how to fish. "Right there, close to shore, just up against that log." And when I'd drop a lure just in the right spot, he'd say, "Well that was a professional cast, honey girl." I'd swell with pride. I never cared if we caught any fish. I just wanted him, to hear him and feel close to him.

A few years before he died, I stopped over at his house on a Saturday afternoon. I hadn't been there long when he abruptly said, "Wait here," and then headed towards the basement. It didn't take long for him to come back up carrying a long cardboard tube. He opened the tube and started handing me pieces of a bamboo fly rod, four in all. I had never seen the rod, didn't know it existed before that day. He told me that his father gave him this rod, and now he was giving it to me. It was brittle, delicate in structure and in meaning. I held it softly. I had no idea that afternoon would be such a momentous one. Before he put two pieces together at their metal fittings, he fixed those bright blue eyes on me and wiped one of the ends on his nose. A natural lubricant to ease the two pieces together and ensure that they could be separated later. He looked at me with intention as he did this. He was giving me the rod, but also a part of our shared history and wanted, needed, to pass it on in the right way. The same way his dad passed it on to him. So, for decades, generations of my kin have wiped their greasy noses on the junctions of that rod. Which is really, really gross. But I didn't mention that at the time, of course. Instead, I returned his gaze with the same light blue eyes I inherited from him, said nothing, and nodded. *I understand.*

It was my love for my grandpap that lead to a deep connection to rivers and lakes. I feel the peace of him whenever I'm in or around water. That combined with my math and science inclinations led to a master's degree in fisheries. My job as Executive Director of an environmental nonprofit, the Bad River Watershed Association, rolled all these traits together. We designed and implemented volunteer monitoring programs for people to study streams near their homes. We brought that data to non-scientists to invest them in understanding how precious those rivers are. We fought for money to protect and restore rivers and created opportunities for citizens to help with restoration. We worked with road crews to take care of both roads and streams when installing culverts.

I was the engine and conductor of the work we did, and I was all in. For years, the work was completely filling, because... I mean... *look* at what we were creating. Even the stresses of a start-up didn't bother me. When I first got hired, I called the then board president after a couple weeks and asked, "So how does a person get paid around here?" He paused and then said slowly, "Good question. You should figure that out next." Oh... Okay! No problem. I loved building this airplane as we were flying it. Loved the accomplishment of jumping every hurdle, even as those hurdles got higher and more frequent. I loved the freedom, that the only thing that could prevent me from initiating my ideas was myself. Could I craft the work to be valuable enough to make a meaningful impact? Could I fund it? Could I get a cadre of supporters behind it? You bet I could. Let's go.

I was the sole staff for a couple years until I raised enough money to bring on a part time volunteer coordinator named Bob. I quickly came to appreciate his thoughtful perspective, dry wit and sincere caring for people. We became fast friends. When he left as a staff member and moved on to board president, it was an easy transition from me being his boss to him becoming mine, because of our mutual respect and enjoyment of each other.

Matt came on about a year later to increase the scientific rigor of our programs. He was rock solid in his technical expertise and approached it with the reserved hesitancy of a scientist: cautious, deliberate, well cited, and somewhat dry on the outside. He had a deep caring for water as well and an inscrutable commitment to details that let me not have to worry about them. Val came on later to de-geek all the great science we were doing. Val was like a big hug. Funny and light and charming. With her science background, she could understand the technical work but was so great at talking with people in a real way that she made it all approachable.

As staff, the three of us were a tight team. We had big titles, crap pay, long work weeks and no job security. The livelihoods of our three families were now counting on my ability to consistently bring in dollars to keep the lights on, a challenge that both excited and scared me. At times we'd secure funding for a year and we'd feel absolutely lavish. Even then, the cash flow was a constant stress. I'd check in with our treasurer, Jim, regularly to see if we could cash our pay checks. I quickly learned to wait after the first answer, since I'd often get a call a twenty minutes later, "Don't cash those checks!" It was easier when I was the only one inconvenienced by this. Having to explain it to Matt and Val made me realize how absurd it was to employ people in this way. But they hung in there, because we loved what we were building for the rivers.

Bob, Matt and Val were some of the first to know about my diagnosis. I'd been in and out of the office just enough to keep things limping along, and I'd give them updates on my procedures and appointments. In two weeks, I would have the primary lump removed, a procedure conveniently called a "lumpectomy." A pre-surgery MRI would look for any other cancer hiding in my chest or armpit. Until then, there was no other cancering to be done. I had only to wait.

As anxious as I was to get started with treatment, the extra few days allowed us the time to figure out a plan for how work would carry on while I was out of the office so much. Bob, Matt, Val and I sat at the conference room in our office. Conference room is a generous description actually. It was a wide spot in the entry way that we crammed a glass topped table that I scrounged from the basement along with a handful of mismatched really uncomfortable chairs. There were no windows, only doors to other offices on all sides, leaving just one wall wide enough for a massive white board that I also scrounged from the basement.

Over the years, we'd spent hours in front of that white board outlining our work, the funding we had in hand, and pending grant requests to figure out how we'd adjust our time to cover all the work. In those meetings, I was the problem solver, the one who laid out options and quickly moved through them. I held the different colored dry erase markers and outlined delivera-bles for our existing programs, their connections to each other and to partners, both now and into the future. As cheerleader and emotional manager, I talked us through uncertainty so that the combination of low pay, high-stress and long days wouldn't make them run out the door in a flash of burnout. I took on my role as Executive Director as part water scientist, part diplo-mat and part accountant delivered with a stand-up comedy and motivational speaker vibe.

But not that day in the hallway/conference room. That day I sat at the back of the table, far away from white board. I didn't pick up the dry erase markers, because I had no capacity to dissect a puzzle. Cancer made it so that I wasn't in the *mood*. I couldn't even manage my own emotions, let alone anyone else's. Four bodies came to the meeting but only three working minds.

Bob took the lead for me, stepped in gently to turn a jagged path into something we could cross. He started writing on that white board with the different colored markers, and I said hardly anything. I sat with my arms folded across my chest and had to work hard to give more than one-word answers. He was trying to balance two things he loved dearly: trout streams and me. The latter was probably only recognized to its full extent with my diagnosis. Bob was trained as a minister, and still held on to the part of pastoring centered on caring for people. I watched as he weighed every word, taking great care not to put pressure on me, but also trying to fulfill his obligation to the rivers and the organization. We both knew this as it was happening, we'd acknowledge it with a held gaze, and then would just keep going. Every once and a while I'd have to say words like "tumor" and "surgery," and it didn't feel possible these words fit around one of us, around me.

During the month before my cancer diagnosis, I had been talking with Bob about my uncertainty about staying on as director. The pressure and stress of it started to wear. Too many hours. Too much constant uncertainty. Too much administrative work and not enough streams work. I was completely torn because I so believed in what we were doing. I couldn't imagine another person taking on my role there because the organization was me. My identity was completely interwoven into everything we did. But I wanted a steady paycheck without having to scrounge up the money for it. I wanted to work a reasonable 40-hour week. But every time I'd even try to describe what it took to keep the organization going, and budget around finding a replacement, the impossibility of it overwhelmed me and slowed all my thoughts to molasses.

But now there we were, with Bob laying out all I did as director on the white board. A scramble of different colored text for different programs, with arrows and boxes and circles to highlight important connections. Details were filled in around the margins, those small things that are so second nature you don't even remember them but turn out are pretty essential—oh you know, like depositing checks. I watched as Bob took on more administrative tasks, wondering if this was the start of the slide out of my director role wondering how I'd get back into this high-speed life again after treatments. But I was unable to image of life after treatments, one thing at a time.

The biggest chunk of that white board was covered in work related to a potential mining project that had recently picked up traction. About a year before my diagnosis, when work problems seemed like the biggest problems, a mining company expressed interest in developing the largest iron ore mine on the planet just south of Ashland. The ore was buried 1,000 feet deep in a ridge called the Penokee Hills, a ridge that ran 30 miles across the headwaters of the watershed we worked in. It was a beautiful mountain of rock outcrops and hardwood forests. Broad wetlands lined the base of the ridge; the rain they collected seeped out as cold water into the trout streams that meandered through them. Eventually, all the water that ran off those hills emptied into Lake Superior, but not before it passed through a massive freshwater estuary on the Bad River Indian Reservation. The Tribe originally settled there to harvest the wild rice as both food and medicine, and they still do. All that water, and the life it supported, was in jeopardy if the mine went in.

There hadn't been any operating mines in the area since the 1950s, which was still recently enough for people to remember the "good old days" of mining, when there were more jobs. A lot of small towns around here - the bars and schools and housing - were built with profits from harvesting ore. One of the local schools claimed the Granite Diggers as their mascot. Another called themselves The Midgets, apparently a show of reverence for shorter workers well-sized to work in the mine shafts?

We moved to northern Wisconsin 2004, so I wasn't part of that history, but being from Pittsburgh, the Iron City, I had some context for mining. In fact, the ore that was harvested from northern Wisconsin decades ago was shipped by rail to Pittsburgh for processing. In the early 1900's, the air in Pittsburgh was thick with the soot of it, and the rivers were trash. When I was a kid, my grandmother took me on a tour of one of the many mansions in Pittsburgh, with walls literally lined in gold, built from the profits of mining. She was enthralled with the art of wealth, but I was more struck by the desperately run-down houses we passed on the way there. I saw that mining made for incredible profits for a few, built on the backs of far more.

Development of the mine was just a zygote of an idea, the developers presenting vague scenarios with promises that mining could now be done responsibly. But in reality, the mining company was in a pinch. To put in the mine, they'd not only dig down through the Penokees, destroying those hills wherever the ore was harvested, they'd also need to fill a massive amount of wetlands with waste rock, and they'd need unlimited access to groundwater for processing. But state laws prevented them from doing those things.

What luck for the mining company a Republican controlled house, senate and governor's office (some reps with hefty donations from the mining company) were more than willing to re-write the mining laws to accommodate them. The narrative the mining company created was one of good paying jobs without any negative impacts to clean water, while behind the scenes dismantling the very regulations that would prevent rivers, wetlands and groundwater from being polluted or destroyed. The legislature put out a bill to loosen mining regulations. And a vote was coming soon.

We'd distributed a petition that simply stated that laws shouldn't be weakened to allow mining companies to pollute. We had 1,400 signatures to deliver to our elected representatives, to convince them to vote against this thing. Before I got cancer, I scheduled a series of meetings with state senators and representatives. I had been planning to make the six-hour drive to Madison, the state capital, with Bob. Now that trip was in question, along with everything else.

We laid out different combinations of staff driving down, postponing the trip or skipping it entirely. I tried to look objectively through our options. But there was part of me that never wanted to go on this trip or to be deeply entrenched in a small-town fight over development and dirty politics and spin doctors. I never aspired to be caught within the contentious paradigm of a polarizing issue and the spokesperson for one of those polarities. It was horribly uncomfortable. As an organization, we had worked so hard to build a nonpartisan coalition with a broad and diverse representation within our community for the last ten years; relationships built on listening to different perspectives, accepting the validity of those perspectives, and finding common ground. That resonated. But in environment versus economics battles, theatrical tactics were the norm to get the attention of a short-memoried and an easily-distracted public. It's not the reasoned, calm conversations that get noticed. Histrionics in a fight to be heard—forced or natural—did not resonate. In fact, I hated it. And there came my cancer diagnosis, a window to make a gracious exit. I could. I could just take this least liked, but maybe most important aspect of my job and push it to the side for a few months. It would be reasonable. Cancer is stressful, fair enough to scale it back a little.

But I couldn't. Because it mattered. I was prepared better than any of us on the content of the bill and the most destructive elements of it. I still felt physically fine. If I skipped it, I would sit around thinking about cancer, or worse, thinking about rivers drying up because I didn't show up big. Life continued to go on, even with a cancer diagnosis, which was baffling and chaotic. I finally looked at Bob and said slowly, "Well... maybe we should just go."

He looked back at me, gave one short nod and waited to see if I'd waiver. I knew that Bob was wondering if this was right for me, if he should intervene on my behalf, because he's that kind of guy. I didn't feel certain about anything, but I held his gaze long enough to convince him that I was decided. We'd go.

With the lobbying trip resolved, we moved on to the rest of my job tasks. I listened and watched as they all took on more to cover for me, even though they were already swamped. I felt so sorry for asking them to do this. So grateful that they took it on so willingly, but I couldn't say anything or else I'd crumble. Instead, I gave them all a quick thanks so I wouldn't get emotional and tried to keep moving.

That white board stayed up after the meeting, my pre-cancer life sketched out thoroughly across it. There was no equivalent white board around the corner for what was to come. It was unmapped, unknown. The contrast was striking. I knew that things were going to change, but I didn't know how. My life had been so overrun by work; I couldn't fathom the possibility of something different.

A few days later, Bob and I rode down to Madison together. In the morning, we had short and forgettable conversations with a few senators and representatives. I felt exceptionally ineffective because I was overwhelmed that I was even there. I had cancer. Right now. But I couldn't feel anything. I knew the words to say, knew they should be delivered with conviction, but I was empty. I wondered if we were accomplishing anything at all.

Our last meeting was with a gruff and curt senator from down state. He was the most likely swing vote. I'd never met him before and was surprised that he kept interrupting me. He dominated the conversation by telling me about the challenges of being a legislator. I listened at first, because I'm polite. But I was getting increasingly annoyed. I did not drive down here in between a cancer diagnosis and surgery to be lectured on everything but the mining bill. Finally, I got pissed enough that I leaned forward and took control of the conversation. Volume a little louder. Eye contact a little more direct. I spoke without breaks so that he couldn't jump back in. But I stayed professional, because the intent was to get him to listen, not to turn him off. He'd try to dominate again, and I'd placate him for a half sentence before redirecting back to the mining legislation. The effects of draining those wetlands. The implications of unlimited access to groundwater. The magnitude of environmental degradation this bill would allow. The better solutions in the protections that the existing law provided. The balance shifted, and we finally started having a conversation. I was on. I was back. After another sixty minutes, he asked me to be on a committee over the next few months to draft better legislation.

With that, I was immediately sucked back into cancer's molasses. I sat back in my chair. Because all I could think about was that I'd probably still be in chemo then. I stared at him blankly and said nothing. Not exactly the end note I would have wanted.

After our scheduled meetings, Bob and I bumped into a colleague outside who offered to take our picture. We ended up posting that picture on the front page of our newsletter, surrounded by an article about the bill and our efforts. I can't even read the article now whenever I look back on it. Because the picture says everything about that trip. We both have pained half smiles, and a hollow expression that I find haunting. Bob has his hands in his pockets, with a shrug as if to say *I can't believe that Michele has cancer and we came down here anyway.* I had been training for a half marathon that summer, so physically I looked fine. It's my expression, and the way I'm holding myself. I looked like an exoskeleton, completely empty. So very different from the engaged, dynamic director I was just a month earlier. I didn't realize then that the picture captured the start of a new life, one that had been eviscerated by cancer and would end up looking very different from the one that preceded it.

Turning a Corner

After the trip to Madison, my reduced work schedule allowed for an obsessive amount of time for cancer research. I began homeschooling myself into a degree in oncology. A degree I sought to earn in three weeks. I'd only feel settled if I felt that I was making exceptionally well-informed decisions, so I dug into learning about breast cancer with the same scientific approach I applied to researching streams. Our best appreciation of the processes of the world comes in small bits that build off other small bits in a cautious and constant quest for understanding. Researchers conduct tests in both laboratory settings and clinical trials. They'll publish papers describing some new nugget of knowledge based on the patterns in the data they collect. In the realm of science, we call all the different papers published in all the different journals "The Literature." We scientists love the literature.

I scoured paper after paper for all things breast cancer: the mechanisms of the disease, treatment options, debates on efficacy and the rationale for dissenting perspectives. I prepared a comprehensive mini review of breast cancer for family and friends across the country to keep us equally informed. It helped us steer clear from the harder conversations about fear. Well, except for that one time that spell check changed lipoma (a benign fatty mass) to lymphoma. That got everyone *really* worried. Oops. I did *not* have lymphoma. Did I mention that I only had three weeks to finish my homeschooled breast cancer thesis?

My review covered the removal of primary tumors, and the margins around the tumor we were seeking to maintain as we sliced that knob from my chest wall. I looked into the error around the biopsy method, and the implications of a potentially different pathology once they extracted the offending tumor. My MRI showed there was only one lump of cancer in there, phew, but I researched what it would mean if there was more, just in case. Jon wasn't as excited as I was about my review. He was more inclined to let the doctors do the doctoring. But he knew that taking action helped me feel in control, so he mustered some enthusiasm about it, even if he never looked at it.

At my next appointment with the surgeon, Jon and I waited with a pile of papers and a long list of questions from my research. We first met her a couple weeks ago and were shocked at how young she looked. Maybe she was just aging extraordinarily well, or maybe she was a female Doogie Howser clocking in at about fifteen. I almost said out loud *You're the surgeon?* But she won me over with her clear and measured explanations, reserved, but with a faint static of electricity.

At this appointment, she talked us through the lumpectomy in detail. A lumpectomy is an outpatient procedure, which I found shocking. Because it was surgery. Cancer surgery. I oscillated between, O*h, wow, such a small deal that it's just an outpatient* *thing* and *Are you freaking kidding me!?* After pulling the primary lump, they'd also look for spread by following the lymphatic system to the first node out from the tumor, called the sentinel node. They'd remove that node and test it mid-surgery for evidence of cancer. The sentinel node is like a gate keeper - the cancer can't spread without getting there first. If it tested negative, we'd all breathe a sigh of relief, or do a little jig, and come up with a bunch of witty ways to say, "My node is negative, baby!" If there was any cancer in that first node though, I'd go back in for another surgery to pull the rest of the lymph nodes under my armpit and test them for cancer as well. I referenced my papers at each step as we talked it through, and she answered my questions with a woven mix of calm and intensity, in a way that made me confident in her. When I read her appointment notes afterward, I saw that she indicated I was "...very well informed." Dang straight sister.

Up until then, I had avoided telling the girls about my cancer diagnosis, because I really, *really* didn't want to. I found it remarkably easy to shove my fear behind a thick mask, so they wouldn't see it. But Jon was gently insistent. *You can't keep running into the basement every time you get a call. More than anyone, they deserve to know.*

I knew that I couldn't manage their emotions as well as my own. I needed them to not be scared of this. But I had the friendly cancer, I reminded myself, so that made it easier. I focused on that as we were sitting around dinner one night and said, in the most nonchalant way, "So girls, I wanted to tell you something. I went to the doctor the other day and they found a little lump in my breast. It has a little cancer in it, so I'm going to have it taken out next week." I played it so cool, like we might be planning a day trip to the county fair. No intense eye contact, no solemn voice.

The girls knew a woman from school who had recently died from cancer. We went to her funeral just last year. I saw Lily's shoulders sag with that memory, with recognition, as she squinted her eyes in worry and asked, "Oh Mama, is it the bad kind?"

"No, no," I said casually. "There are different kinds of cancer. Mine isn't a bad kind. Lumps like this happen sometimes. They're just going to pull it out and it'll be fine. I'm going to have some extra treatments after that, just to be sure." I shrugged indifference, "I might be a little tired and grumpy, but it's okay. It's just the way you do things when this happens."

They were studying me to see if they could buy it. It was amazing how easy it was to act this part. I served myself another helping of dinner, moving on.

They did buy it. Another mom from their school told me that Caitlin seemed so unaffected when she said, "Oh yea! My mom has cancer. But they're going to take it out and she'll be fine." Perfect.

We spent the next week preoccupied with getting ready for Halloween. My mom came out from Denver for the surgery, eager to help and also just to be near me. She helped prepare the girls' costumes for trick or treating and arranged for our neighbors to take the girls for the night. I'd wear a gown as a costume for Halloween, hoping, in the true spirit of the holiday, that it would be sufficient enough to ward off ghosts. It was a very long week.

Surgery day was consumed by awaiting post-op results. The lumpectomy no longer concerned me; that I was having surgery at all had been diminished to a side note. The status of the sentinel node held main title to the day. I was wheeled to the radiology department, dressed only in ghost-averting gown, for a nuclear injection in my breast that would track the location of that sentinel node. The fully dressed people in the hospital avoided looking at me. I was invisible. When I was the dressed patient, I too looked away from gowned patients in wheelchairs, thinking I was offering privacy. But I now realized it was fear of whatever ailed them. Looking away would keep me further from it. I made small talk with my escort so that everyone could hear that a real live person was in that chair.

I envisioned the guards at my gate-keeper node as they injected radioactive liquid, hotter than lava, into my breast. *Find that node*, I thought. *See if those guards have been at constant attention.*

Moments later, in the pre-operative room with another handful of patients, I stared at the ceiling trying to ignore the scorching pain in my chest. I tried not to ignore the doctor on the other side of a curtain tell his patient her surgery would be "the easiest of the day." I tried harder not to resent them both for hearing it. Any moment, they'd all be listening to the overview of my surgery when they'd likely think, *Yikes, I'm glad I'm not her.* I closed my eyes and thought gate keepers and clean margins. That's all I needed.

The next thing I knew was being rolled back to the recovery room, flashes of white pulsating as I was pushed down the hallway under the lights. So fast. Why was he pushing me so fast? I kept my eyes closed and managed to get out in a whisper, "Margins?"

I heard the man from above and behind me, "Yes. Clear margins."

"Node." I slurred. "Was the node clear?"

"Yes. Your node was clear, too."

Elation within an anesthetic haze is severely limited. Had I heard this news with all my faculties, my reaction would have been epic. I *felt* epic. I clenched my hand in to a fist and lifted it straight above me, just as we rounded a corner that rolled me into the side rails. "Whoa...what are you doing there?" asked my escort.

"Hold on," I managed. He slowed as I lifted my hand back up, made the fist again and pulled it back towards my body with a long, extended "Yesssssss." A slow-motion fist bump was all I had in me. Friendly cancer removed, I'd have this behind me in no time. Maybe even without chemotherapy. I finished off my celebration with a very sleepy "My node... is... negative... baby." I was in the clear.

I was having a hard time pulling out of the anesthesia, so Jon and my mom watched me sleep and wake in the soft light of the recovery room. Despite the news of a clear node, my mom was still tormented by seeing her daughter in a post-surgery stupor. This was the woman who bought me twenty bars of antiseptic soap before my surgery. The surgeon told me the specific kind of soap to get to prevent infection. Well if one bar of soap would help me, Mom had clearly figured a case would be miracle-working. Mom had also brought a shirt with a wide-open neck, so that I could get in and out of it with my limited range of motion post-surgery. I didn't even know I'd need a shirt like that, but she did. She'd been up for weeks thinking of every detail to find ways to make this easier for me. I told her the shirt fit well, and she bought me another three of them and shook her head with regret at not buying me three more.

Mom and I had talked on the phone almost daily for the past month. She was well aware of every new development, but this was the first time she saw me as a patient with a very serious illness. What I remember most was her quietness. My mom is usually a chatterbox. She loves to talk. Loves to laugh. She is a non-stop flow of pleasant rambling. Jon says that my mom can make a story out of buying a biscuit. When she's really got a good one going, she'll tee it up with a patented, "Oh... My... God..."

"You won't believe this, Michele. Did I tell you about my trip to the grocery store yesterday? Oh... My... God..."

She rarely finishes a sentence when she's wound up on a good yarn, so it's hard to tell what is digression and what is the main narrative. You had better pay attention if you want to know what happened at the grocery store.

"The traffic... it was...I mean you've been on Boyle...I couldn't even believe it... Well...it's the people moving to Denver every day! It's like 10,000 a month... It's crazy. Crazy... It's like that farm. I can't believe it.... There are five different condos up there now. Five! Anyway Michele, the parking lot was full. I mean *full*. I drove around. Oh. My. God. At least three times..."

I can call Mom any time of day and be greeted with a steady chorus of chatter. Her rapid-fire incessant rattling is my lullaby. I'm carried away with her stories, the details of which I hardly ever remember, but it doesn't matter. It's the singsong intonation of her voice, and the familiarity of conversation about nothing that lulls me into such comfort.

But now. She was not chatting now. She was quiet, folding the top sheet over in the dim light, making it even all the way across. She looked like she wanted to tuck it under me, to swaddle me, or better yet crawl into the bed next to me and squeeze me with all her might. But instead, she went back to folding and refolding the sheet, fidgeting until they kicked us out early that afternoon.

A few days later, Mom and I were on our way back from errands when I received a call from my surgeon. I felt a rush of adrenaline. She was calling to tell me the results of the full node pathology. It was rare for follow up testing to yield different results that the mid surgery ones. But it was possible. She kept her calm quiet manner as she told me that the tumor was entirely grade three carcinoma. Different from the mucinous carcinoma of the original sample, this was the aggressively spreading kind of cancer. And then she told me that sentinel node wasn't clear. I recanted my fist bump and went completely numb. I fumbled through some dry, "Thanks for calling," and hung up as soon as I could. I recapped the conversation to my mom in a completely emotionless voice, and we both stared straight ahead the rest of the way home. This was bad news. This meant cancer was in my lymphatic system. That meant it had spread. How far was the question.

That stretch of road has become a black hole of sorts since then. It has become "that corner." The corner where everything changed. The corner to be avoided at all costs.

Jon

Posted by Jon Wheeler, November 7, 2011

After a long day in Duluth, Michele and her Mom made it back home at about 9:00 tonight. I know she is happy to be home. In the morning she'll get to see the kids for a bit which will be a balancing act of keeping them engaged, while trying to keep them at least arms distance from the Mom they dearly love. Tomorrow, we head back up to Duluth to meet with a variety of doctors and discuss possible treatment scenarios. Conclusive test results (expected on Wednesday...) of the axillary nodes that were removed today will influence what treatment is suggested. So, it looks like tomorrow's meetings will involve a lot of "if this, then this..." conversations. All this waiting for answers is tough, but a more certain path should be laid out here soon.

Thanks to everybody for all your love and kindness,
Jon

J on wrote the update because I was too upset to face it. The switch in diagnosis from friendly to aggressive cancer left me too scared to talk. Jon's attentiveness, his instinctive knowing of when I needed support, and when I'd prefer to take the lead, has been a constant in our relationship. I didn't realize it fully, though, until we started navigating cancer together.

Jon and I met eleven years earlier in the fall of 2000. At 26 years old, I moved to Forks, Washington, on the western coast of the Olympic Peninsula. Olympic National Park covers the middle portion of the peninsula, and a lone road circles its coastal edge. Forks is a town of maybe a couple thousand, and once you leave the six blocks of "downtown," you can drive for hours in either direction and only pass a couple small villages. With nearly 100 inches of rain each year and temps that rarely dip below freezing, the forests are remarkably thick and lush. Douglas firs tower hundreds of feet tall, and the duff on the forest floor can swallow you. It is truly remote.

I moved to Forks for a research assistant position at a University of Washington field station. Forks wasn't exactly welcoming to outsiders, even less so to any one of the "ologists" who had ruined the timber industry that had sustained them for decades. I stayed in the research center housing for a very lonely first few weeks.

I took my dog out for a walk on the trails around the field station one day and noticed a dark blue, beat-up VW van parked at the center again. I'd met the other researchers staying at the field station, but not the owner of the van. I was curious about its driver, eager for the possibility of meeting any new friend.

Shortly after I started on the trail, I had to go to the bathroom, so I took a few steps off the trail and found a moderately-hidden spot behind some shrubs. Just as I finished buttoning myself back up, this guy wearing rough jeans and red suspenders with "FORKS" written on them ducked under the bushes. We found ourselves face to face. He was cute, but he had on FORKS suspenders. The people of Forks really despised biologists. Was he a Forks local? Who the hell was this guy?

"Hey," I said, direct and not friendly. "Who are you?"

"Oh hi. I'm Jon," he replied with ease and a faint smile.

"What are you doing out here?" I asked, suspiciously, not sure whether cutie-face-suspender guy had been watching me pee or not.

"I have some friends that stay in the housing here. Just came out to say hi and thought I'd take a walk," he said. So he's friendly with "ologists."

"Where are you from?" I continued to grill him without smiling.

"I grew up in eastern New York State." Hmmm. Not a Forks local, then. An east coaster like myself. "I moved out here to do trail work with the WCC. Right now, we're doing stream restoration stuff."

"How do you like that?" I asked, warming up to him but still not smiling. I knew that the WCC was the Washington Conservation Corps, which is kind of like a domestic Peace Corps. I had just finished a two year stretch of service in a similar program in Oregon.

"It's kind of like playing God in the stream, and I don't know what I think about that."

Here's the thing about Jon. He is so completely himself all the time. He embodies "what you see is what you get." He exudes kindness with absolute sincerity, always. He's interested in how people think, and he's comfortable telling you exactly what he thinks, regardless of whether you're in agreement. I could feel that in these first few sentences. I liked him. I found him interesting. Did I mention that he's really cute?

"Want to go have a beer?" I asked him. Of course, he did.

Our first date

We walked through the woods back towards the research center, a series of buildings in a U-shape. There was a large, grassy open space in the middle of the U, with offices and labs on one side and a handful of small single-story apartments lining the other half. Most of the apartments were vacant, but sometimes students from the Seattle campus would stay short-term to do fieldwork.

A couple of college-aged women were in the unit next to mine while they did spotted owl research in the old growth forests of the peninsula. For years I had been bouncing around the Pacific Northwest, moving from one small, remote town to another, following short-term jobs in fisheries and water science. I was comfortable with the routine. We natural resources folks are usually a tight knit bunch in these types of towns. We find comradery in being the outsiders among long-time townies. I had been trying to befriend my two neighbors since I moved in. I'd try to start conversation whenever I saw them outside our apartments. They seemed fiercely shy. I kept trying, "Hey there, I just picked up some beers, want one?" but they turned me down every time. Oh well.

Since my neighbors didn't want any of the beers I offered (and kept offering), I still had a few in the fridge when Jon and I walked out of the woods that day. I grabbed a couple, glad to just have someone to talk to after weeks of solitude. Jon and I cracked them open on the lawn outside my apartment and hung out like old friends, talking about nothing important, nothing deep. Just easy conversation about the day. It was notable that I felt so comfortable with this guy I just met.

My neighbors walked by a little while later. I chatted them up again because I'm friendly. And Jon did too; it seemed like he had met them before. But this time, my neighbors weren't too busy. They actually talked back! *Oh, I see how it is. Cute guy on the lawn, and suddenly we're all friends.* An hour later, we were planning a potluck dinner. Jon said he'd be right back and headed off into the woods, returning about 15 minutes later with a huge pile of wild mushrooms and a big grin on his face. I was entertained by how pleased he was with himself, yet without ego. He told us all about the different wild mushrooms he liked to harvest. Which ones were in season right now, his favorites, the best ways to cook them. He was good at it. Sautéed, they were delicious.

After dinner in the neighbor's apartment, Jon and I exchanged slightly awkward goodbyes.

"It was nice bumping into you," I said, trying to sound more casual than I felt.

"Yea, maybe I'll bump into you again some time," Jon replied, also trying to sound like he wasn't totally into me. He was totally into me. I could tell.

"Okay, Yea. Sounds good." I stalled.

"See ya," he stalled. We grinned at each other.

As soon as he left, the two neighbors couldn't contain themselves any longer. They sat smitten, talking about how incredibly awesome Jon was.

"He's just so *interesting*. I mean, he's done *everything*. Have you seen any of the flutes he's made?"

"I've seen the knives that he makes. They're really impressive."
They went on.... and on... I was *interested*.

By the way, he wasn't watching me pee that first day we met.
I feel the need to make that clear.

Our second date

A couple days later, Jon and I took a canoe down the Quileute
River. We set out to run a handful of miles and finish up at his
place, a rented trailer along the river just a few miles upstream
from the Pacific Ocean. The Quileute is fed from both rainwa-
ter (seriously, it's *always* raining in Forks) and from the glaciers
on the mountains. It's an absolutely beautiful river that flows
crystal clear over large boulders and clean gravel. As we put the
canoe in, I asked him if he wanted the front or back of the boat.

He paused and said, "Um, yeah, I'll take the back." I didn't
know this yet, but Jon is an extraordinary paddler. Mostly a kay-
aker, but he's skilled in any watercraft. He's guided rafts in Class
V rapids in Maine and spent years paddling big water in Idaho,
and throughout the southeast. He's a "Hey! It's flooding! Let's
go paddle!" kind of guy. It's his thing, and it defined a big part
of him for many years.

We headed downstream in a swift but rapidless current and
passed a few fisherman enjoying the broad, winding bends of
the river. It wasn't long before we started getting into some
rapids—small at first, but they got more exciting pretty quickly
when the waves in the rapids started reaching two to three feet.
When the first wave of 50-degree water poured over me I froze
in shock. "Paddle on your right, Michele!" shouted Jon from

the back of the boat. I started paddling again as the waves kept coming, one after another onto my lap. My mind was singularly filled with only *Holy shit that's cold.* Icy river water kept filling the canoe until I heard Jon behind me, oddly calm.

"Well, Michele... I think we're going to swamp the boat."

We nearly did. We got through the rapids with only a few inches to spare until our canoe would have been completely underwater. We limped to shore and heaved up the canoe to dump the water out. Jon seemed totally unfazed as he readied the boat to keep going. I looked downstream before stepping back in, weary of the waves to come. With the river moving so fast, paddling back upstream wasn't an option. The forest was so thick that hiking back up wasn't an option either. Downstream was the only way to go. I looked to Jon, so relaxed, holding the boat steady and calmly waiting with that easy grin. I put my fate in his hands and climbed back into the front of the boat.

After another few minutes of paddling, we hit another wave train and pulled over to dump water out of the boat again. Then another wave train and stopped to dump the boat. Then another...you get the idea. After the fifth or sixth time, I was so cold I could hardly move. I was bracing myself to pick the boat up when Jon's voice broke through, quiet and kind.

"It's okay. I'll get it."

I wanted to help, but the cold made me clumsy and slow. Jon lifted the boat himself as I stood there shivering. I was in tough-it-out mode at this point. I did not love it. Jon on the other hand seemed completely comfortable. He kept talking, kept his tone light as he stood in the boat to scout each rapid and then expertly guided us through the best line.

In a lull between rapids, Jon said, "Well, Michele, the good thing about this trip is that we'll get to know each other. When things aren't going well, you see what people are really about. For instance, today I learned that when you're upset you get really quiet."

I grinned in the front of the boat and kept paddling quietly, feeling oddly seen. And what I saw in Jon that day is that when things are really difficult, when most people are at their worst, Jon is at his best. Challenge for Jon isn't a negative thing, because it gives him a chance to conquer it. The more intense things get, the better. It feeds him.

By the time we reached his spot on the shoreline, it was close to dark. I was rigid with cold by that point, like the Tin Man from Wizard of Oz. Jon's landlady, Bonnie, led me to their bathroom for a shower and handed me some sweats to change into. Teeth chattering, I nodded my thanks and closed myself in the bathroom. My hands could barely work. I had never been this cold. I stood in the shower letting the warm water run all over me. It was glorious that shower. I turned it up hotter and hotter. It warmed my skin but couldn't touch the cold in my core. I could have stayed there for hours. But remembering I was in someone else's house, I reluctantly finished up and got into the cozy sweats as fast as I could.

When I entered the dining room, Jon was there with a beer in his hand and a big smile on his face talking with Bonnie and her boyfriend, Mike. They were all laughing as Jon recounted parts of our paddle. He handed me a beer and pulled out a chair next to him as he talked. I slipped easily into the conversation as we recreated our trip for them: every wave, every irritation (for me, no irritations for Jon), every bend in the river. We alternated between talking right to each other and bringing Bonnie and Mike back into the conversation. After another ten minutes, I didn't feel cold anymore.

Our third date

A couple days later, (yes, I went back for more) Jon asked me to go for a hike to a special spot he said he'd found in the forest. I'd walked many miles through the woods of the Pacific Northwest. Before coming to Forks, I'd lived in Oregon in the foothills of Mount Hood for a few years. Fisheries surveys for work sent me down miles of streams. Weekends were spent hiking miles through the National Forest. To this day, taking a long walk in the woods one of my very favorite things to do.

Shortly after we set out, we left the trail and started bush-whacking, with Jon leading the way. The woods on the Olympic Peninsula are exceptionally thick, and I fought with big leaf maple and ferns as we walked. The vegetation cleared, and we came up on an enormous wetland. It was beautiful, a mixture of open water and emergent vegetation, bordered by the tall coni-fers at its edges. I took it all in thinking this was the special spot. Then, Jon nodded his head towards the water and said, "Ready?"

I looked at the wetland, and then back at Jon. I mean, I'm a water girl. I've spent lots of time in rivers and wetlands. But I'm usually dressed for wading when I go tromping around in them. I looked down at my jeans, at my heavy readily-water-logged hiking boots and looked back to Jon. I was confused, "You want to... go in there... like this?"

"Yeah," he said with an eager grin, like there wouldn't be any reason not to. "It's really beautiful on the other side, and it's too far to walk around to get to it."

It's the way Jon looks at you. His excitement is so palpable, it's impossible not to catch it. "Okay," I agreed. At first, I tried to stay on top of hummocks, but it soon became pointless. We were full-on wading, without being able to see six inches into the dark water. We reached the middle and the water was up to my armpits. At least it wasn't so cold this time. I hauled my heavy boots forward cautiously, feeling for down logs with each step, hoping I'd avoid a stumble that would fully submerge me. Once I accepted that I was going to be wet, it was really kind of fun. I made an attempt to wring myself out on the other side, while Jon just let himself drip dry, and we headed deeper into the woods.

There is a certain peace in the remoteness of the Olympic temperate rainforest. Some parts of the Olympics get a lot of visitors, but far more of it rarely sees the footprints of people. Sound is buffered by the dense vegetation. Every shade of green blankets every place around you. It's never stormy, no lightning, no torrential downpour. Just a steady rain and a constant stillness that feels eternally a hundred years old. The further away from the beaten path you get, the more that feeling seeps into your bones. It is a wonderful feeling, that steady calm.

We walked without talking, absorbing this place. Jon continued to lead the way, exploring the woods on his own, but always within sight. He didn't baby me on the trek, which would have pissed me off, but offered a hand when I needed help climbing over a log six feet in diameter. He seemed intuitively to know when to help and when to give me space. I could tell that he always knew exactly where I was. It was a comforting feeling, being with someone who knew I was capable, but was also unwaveringly attentive.

Eleven years later, our 756th date

In my second surgery, they removed all the lymph nodes under my armpit. The lymph system carries lots of fluid, and when you pull the rest of the lymph nodes from your armpit, the fluid needs somewhere to go. To allow for that drainage, a two-foot hose had been stitched into my underarm, ending in a soft, three-inch clear ball that was pinned to my pants and collected the draining mixture of blood and lymphatic fluid. Yes, it was as disgusting as it sounds.

Jon helped me love up the girls when I got home while keeping them from jumping all over me. It was about dinner time. I pushed food around on my plate while the rest of my family ate and listened to the girls tell me all their stories from the day. I watched their eyes, big and bright, relieved that we wouldn't be talking about lymph nodes. Their joy about the best markers and how great crayons were for shading was an enormously welcome distraction.

After dinner, I eased myself up to go to the bathroom. Behind the closed door, I lifted my shirt, intrigued by the new hose apparatus sticking out of my arm in the mirror. As soon as I looked at it, I got dizzy and had to hold on to the side of the sink. I started to sweat and felt nausea overwhelm me, a reaction that was totally unexpected. *Uh oh*, I thought. *I might crap myself.* But that fluid ball was attached to my pants and I couldn't pull them down. If I detached the fluid ball, they said, I had to be careful not to let it tug on the stitches. Because if they came out, that would be bad. I closed my eyes and held on tighter to the sink. I was in a pickle.

I said the only thing that came to mine, "Jon." There wasn't a lot of volume, but there didn't need to be. He was there in an instant and helped me get on the pot, with a bucket in case I threw up, and held that fluid ball for me. always had, watching a little more closely for when I need a hand.

At that moment, I was not hot. I mean, "...in sickness and in health," but I didn't think he'd have to do something like this until I was old, not at age thirty-seven. I felt gross. And I felt weak.

"I feel humiliated," I muttered with my head in my hands and sweat pouring off my face.

"Are you all set?" he asked. I nodded.

"Do you want a little time to yourself?" I nodded.

"I'll be right outside when you're ready."

Jon brought the best of himself to helping me with cancer. He treated me as he always had but paid a little closer attention. Just like when we walked through the dense forests of the Olympics, he knew when to offer a hand and when to let me manage on my own.

The next day, he dug through my sewing stuff and found some fabric, thread, and a random needle to sew a little fluid sack satchel for me. He sized a long strap I could wear over my shoulder so that the pouch would sit just above my hip. It held that ball of ick so that I didn't have to look at it. So that I wouldn't end up in another pickle. He stayed two steps away without making me feel like he was watching over me. I knew it as soon as I met him. I scored when I landed this guy. You could not ask for more.

Mihailo

Essentia Health and Dr. Lalich

One day out of the second surgery, Jon and I headed back to Duluth to discuss treatment steps. Medical professionals who live this world every day are accustomed to seeing patients on this timescale. I found it incredible. *Did you people know I had surgery yesterday? Yesterday! And look at me, I'm up and about.* I showed off the fluid sack satchel Jon made to everyone I talked to. I stayed close to Jon's side all day.

In a conventional approach to cancer, the location and distribution of cancer throughout the body is an essential bit of information. The extent of spread is referred to as "staging," indicated as a number between 0 and IV. The assigned staging number correlates with likelihood of survival and guides decision-making regarding treatment options. For breast cancer, the number of cancerous lymph nodes near the breast and under the armpit determine staging. If just a few of the nodes were cancerous, I'd get a low number, which would be good. If many were cancerous, it would indicate that more of the cancer was on the move, a scarier cancer. This was the day we would get those results, and therefore the treatment plan.

Our first appointment was with Dr. Mihailo Lalich. He was Dr. Lalich at the time, but through years of cancering together, he's become Mihailo. I butchered his name for years, and he never even flinched. This says so much about Mihailo, about who he sees as the important person in the conversation. It wasn't until I finally asked how to say his name that he demonstrated by pointing to himself (ME), pointing up (HIGH) and then down (LOW).

Jon and I were still in shock during that first appointment. The past couple weeks had been a roller coaster of *Oh shit, cancer! Phew, it's the friendly cancer that doesn't spread...Great news! It didn't spread!... Oh wait. It did spread, and it's not friendly.* We were numb, and we were scared. In the past couple of days, we had exhausted all the *what ifs*, with each other and our families. There was nothing else to talk about. We just waited.

Dr. Lalich entered the room after a slight knock. He wasn't wearing the requisite white lab coat, just tan slacks with a button-up shirt. We seemed about the same age. Could a competent cancer doctor be about my age?

"Hi. Michele?" he said and shook my hand. Turned to shake Jon's hand as well. We started talking as though a mutual friend just introduced us, and he was genuinely interested in getting to know us. We were twenty minutes in, and the word "cancer" hadn't even entered the room yet. He made us feel comfortable. He made us feel like he knew that we were real people and that we mattered. He made the room not feel so cold.

At a natural break in the conversation, Dr. Lalich transitioned seamlessly to discussion of treatment options. We talked through my status. Yesterday's surgery removed seventeen lymph nodes in all. Two had come back positive for cancer, one measured 1.1 cm in diameter, the other 0.8 cm. Those seemed big to me. *Observable*. How did the mammogram miss them? *And the MRI*? I mean a centimeter is as big as a marble. Medical tests, like all science, are imperfect. This was hard to accept in studying streams and rivers, but even harder here. Including the sentinel node, I was at a total of three positive nodes: Stage II cancer.

Dr. Lalich presented the options he and a team of doctors— MRI specialists, surgeons, nursing staff, radiologists and oncologists—debated as my best treatment. For the chemotherapy phase, they debated two different options. Both used the chemo drug Cytoxan, but one treatment mixed in another chemo drug called Taxotere (the TC option) and the other mixed in Adriamycin (the AC option). The performance of both cocktails was similar, but the AC version was more aggressive, with a very slight increase in survival. Both had a long and similar list of potential side effects, but the AC option included potential damage to heart muscle. Given my young age, the Essentia team recommended TC. I had a lot of years left to rely on my ticker. They wanted to protect those years.

I hammered Dr. Lalich with questions. I asked about the pros and cons, the risks associated with each treatment. Every time he answered, I pressed for more information. When I did, he would say, "That's a good question," as if he was glad I asked, and then he'd explain calmly and completely. He'd use the big words, but then made sure I understood them. When he described a body of research on any aspect of the treatment,

I asked for a reference and he'd print it off immediately. I was getting the details I needed to take charge of this, instead of succumbing to it. It was the only way I could feel like myself.

At one point, Dr. Lalich tilted the computer screen towards me to show me diagrams of survival rates associated with the different treatment options. If I chose to do no follow-up treatment, I had a 50 percent chance of surviving for the next five years. With chemo, my change of surviving the next five years increased to around 70 percent. With radiation, it was 80 percent. With hormonal therapy, 90 percent. In the world of cancer treatment, these are very good numbers. But as I looked at the graphs, all I could think about was that I could be that one in ten breast cancer patients who didn't make it five more years, even with the max amount of treatment. It stopped me cold.

The eager banter of two scientists looking at data disappeared. That graph of survival rates terrified me. It changed me quickly from scientist to patient, so much so that I couldn't speak. When Dr. Lalich asked if I wanted a copy of this data, I declined, quietly. He seemed to recognize the shift, nodded slightly, and clicked to another screen, not adding that printout to my growing stack.

After a slight knock on the door, a nurse peeked in to let us know that I was over 40 minutes late for my appointment with the radiation oncologist. Dr. Lalich thanked her and calmly turned back to me. "What other questions do you have?" That was when I fully saw him. Even when pressured, he was fully present and made no effort to rush until all our questions were answered. He talked to us like we were his only patients, like what happened to me mattered; it was enormously comforting.

After nearly two hours, we started to wrap it up only when my list of questions was exhausted. The Essentia Team had made their recommendation, but Dr. Lalich made it clear that he was open to my input. This was my treatment and so my decision. I looked to Jon for the first time during the appointment. He returned my gaze and waited. I felt paralyzed. On one hand, I needed to be in charge of my own ship. But on the flip side, how could I make *this* decision? I needed more info, another perspective. I needed a second opinion.

Mayo Clinic

Fortunately, we live only about five hours away from the Mayo Clinic in Rochester, MN. I'm talking *the* Mayo Clinic. If there were any cutting-edge therapies as options, we'd find them there. Mom and I made the drive to Mayo three days later, while Jon stayed home with the girls.

Mayo Clinic is spread throughout most of downtown Rochester. It kind of *is* the city of Rochester. It took a few attempts and some doubling back before we found our building and entered into a massive, four-story atrium encased in glass. The sound of classical music from a grand piano filled the room, a false calm in an inherently intense space. The dichotomy grated on me like insincerity. People moved in every direction. Some were in wheelchairs. Some were tethered to oxygen tanks that they wheeled behind them on little carts. Some moved quickly with intention. Others shuffled slowly looking as lost as I felt. This, I realized with a startling sense of clarity, was a slice of life that most people don't experience. I wasn't the only one who had recently heard bad news and drastically shifted every aspect of my life to deal with it. It was palpable being surrounded by illness and will, fear and hope. I was filled with the feeling that we were all in this together.

We spent the morning getting shuffled throughout the building for one test after another, ushered through each department with pinpoint efficiency. By late afternoon, we made it up to the breast center, the star event. Mom and I were led to an exam room not very different from the one Jon and I had been in just a few days before. I adjusted my fluid sack satchel so that we could sit together on a two-person bench, and we waited.

A few minutes later the doctor came in. He had a strong build, maybe six feet tall, and did wear the requisite white lab coat. After brief introductions, he sat across from us and leaned forward, elbows on his knees, as he talked through my test results and staging status. His recommendation was to go with the AC version of chemo.

I asked about my age, as one of the deciding factors in in Essentia's recommendation to go the TC route, and he said "It is *also* because of your age that I recommend the AC chemotherapy. You have a long life to live. I would recommend the more aggressive option to help you treat your cancer."

Different recommendation, same reason. The questions started to pile up again. *Why? What if? What about?* No, the difference between the two wasn't that great, but he stuck by his recommendation. No, there wouldn't be any advantage in getting treatment here at Mayo. I could get the same meds at either cancer center. We had spent hardly fifteen minutes with the Mayo doctor when I saw him glance at his watch. It was a subtle move, but compared to my appointment with Dr. Lalich, where time stopped until all my questions were fully answered, it felt drastic.

I realized in his twist of the wrist that my expectations of this appointment had been far off base. I wanted the doctors at Mayo to put me at the center of their world—even just for an hour—and bring all the Mayo resources to bear on my diagnosis and treatment. I wanted to feel 100 percent confident in which of these two poison cocktails to infuse into my body repeatedly, to know I was making The Right Choice. With that glance at his watch, I saw more clearly what we had signed up for: a professional opinion. We got it. The decision was still mine. And it was time to go.

Mom and I talked options as we drove to Minneapolis for her flight back to Denver. For next few days, I talked through the decision over and over with close friends, my sister, my dad, and Jon. I kept waiting for one of them to say, "AC is the way to go, definitely" or even an "I think I'd go with TC." But no one did. It was too heavy a choice to make. The consequences too important, too dire. No one would touch it. Instead I heard, "That's a hard decision. What do you think you're going to do?" I was on my own here. Even with the love and support and hours of conversation, I still felt enormously isolated. I'm the one who has cancer, so I'm the one who has to pick. *Just pick one!*

It turned out my scientific approach - to fully invest in the literature and all the knowledge it provides - wasn't going to work. My attempt at a homeschooled degree in oncology only led to a limitless number of new questions. Instead, I decided to go with the option that felt right. Yes, I trust my gut, but facts and data weigh heavily in my deliberation. This time I was lending more credence to process. Essentia took time with me and considered my case as a team. There was more than one head lending his or her insight towards a collective recommendation, and more time spent thinking though what to do. In contrast, the Mayo appointment was the opinion of one oncologist made with about fifteen minutes of consideration. My final choice was based on my trust in the process at Essentia. This was a new thing for me.

With a Little Help from my Friends

I was getting used to having cancer and the conversations that it brings. Talking about survival rates became less shocking and more pragmatic. I was becoming accustomed to my fluid sack, almost. Jon's hand-stitched satchel made it easier for me to deal with it. But I wanted a shower, at least a bath. My range of motion was limited with the tube still stitched into my side. More so I was worried that one look at that tube full of bloody fluid might dizzy me to the ground again like the night I came home from surgery. I'm not typically a fainter. That I nearly did made me wary of showering on my own.

I could ask Jon for help. I knew he would help me without hesitation. I knew he would make my discomfort more bearable just like he did when we were canoeing the Quileute. Feeling so vulnerable and gross during that last fluid sack incident was still with me. I didn't want any more of that. So, I called Autumn.

At a half mile down the road, Autumn and Chris were some of our closest neighbors. They went to college with Jon fifteen years ago and had been here ever since. When Jon introduced me to Autumn, I held one of my girls, only six months old at the time. Autumn held her son Caleb, who was just a month older. We rocked our babies back and forth as we talked about our pregnancies. We let our kids down when they started to squirm and talked about our births. We picked them up again when they reached for us and talked about early infant stages. We've continued balancing kids and conversation ever since. We are family.

Chris and Jon were both stay-at-home dads when our kids were young. They took the kids on "Dad-ventures" together regularly, swimming and canoeing and searching for turtles. Their son Caleb came to stay with us when Autumn went into labor with their second son, Danny. When she had her daughter Nora a few years later, we whooped with joy that her little scrumpet was a girl. We share holidays together, with routines carved out into tradition. Autumn makes the pies. I make the gravy, etc. She is my closest friend here.

Autumn is also a registered nurse, a handy friend to have when you have medical stuff going on. Since my diagnosis, she had been my sounding board for all things cancer. I called and asked for her help bathing. Even though we were so close, it was weird. I didn't like it, which Autumn responded to in a very Autumn-like way. She paid little attention to how uncomfortable it was for me to ask for her help with a bath to not give it any more weight. She came right over.

She walked in without knocking as she always did. Autumn is a little thing. In her five-foot four frame, she's adorable. What she lacks in height she makes up for in energy; she's a bustle of activity. Our first floor was a large open space. From my spot on the couch nestled in the opposite corner, I watched her kick off her boots and unlayer all of her winter wear, chatting lightly as she hustled a pot of soup over to the fridge. Autumn's soups were famous in my house. Lil and Caitlin loved everything she made. They'd be happy with dinner tonight. There was something reassuring about seeing her walk in my house in a flurry, not with nervous energy, just because she's Autumn. She made an icky moment feel normal.

After a few minutes of chit chat, she took in a breath and raised her eyebrows at me, "Well, should we do this?" gesture. I stammered my needs again reluctantly, my concerns about tugging the tube and passing out. I looked at her and shrugged an "awkward!" She acknowledged that with a curt nod and said casually, "When I was in nursing school, I had to practice giving someone a bath. A friend of mine agreed to let me practice with him. How about we just pretend like you're helping me practice for nursing school?" Oh Autumn. Yes, let's do that. I felt myself relax.

We talked about the kids while we waited for the tub to fill. We talked about her job and mine as she washed my hair. She kept chit-chatting as she deftly managed the ick ball. I knew she wouldn't let it drop or tug. So I didn't have to look at it or think about it at all. When we were done, she helped me get settled in back in the living room. She hustled back to my laundry room and shifted a load from washer to dryer, returning seconds with her hands on her hips, taking stock. Dinner was ready; laundry was taken care of; I was clean and comfortable. Satisfied, she started layering her winter gear to leave. "Alright, the kids will be home soon, so I'm gonna go. See you later. Love you!" She hustled out the door. Autumn. Thank you.

A few days later, I needed her again. I was soon to start chemo and decided to prep for complete hair loss by getting a super short cut. My co-worker, Val went with me for my haircut. She set up an appointment for herself to get a shorter doo in solidarity. Afterwards we were going to scarf party that Autumn set up at a local brew pub. She invited a bunch of friends to bring head scarves so I could try on a bunch of different colors, patterns, and styles. We'd make it fun so that it was bearable. It seemed like good prep for baldness at the time.

Val and I walked into a salon that I had been to a few times before. The stylist was another neighbor. She knew my story and knew the reason for this haircut. Like I said, everyone knows everyone around here. I told her that I wanted it nearly shaved in the back and about an inch or two on the top.

She said, "Well you're actually going to do something different this time," which made me smile. I had essentially the same hairstyle since I was sixteen years old. My thick, dark brown hair was all one length, falling to about mid-back. My raciest haircut over the past 25 years shortened it to—gasp! —above my shoulders. This was a big haircut in style, but even bigger in purpose.

When the first clump of hair ten inches long hit the ground, I felt my heart sink. My hair. She kept cutting. Val gave me encouraging smiles. I watched in the mirror as the stylist clipped away, and my hair kept hitting the ground. She turned me away from the mirror to put a bunch of styling crap in my hair. Just the smell of that goo made me gag. I never used styling crap. The stylist coaxed it this way and that with a blow dryer. When she spun me around to see the finished product in the mirror, I found myself staring at my Uncle Don in the mirror. Don't get me wrong, my Uncle Don is a fine-looking man. But he's a *man*. As Val and the stylist gushed about how great the new cut looked, I could feel the tears start to well. I stifled them and watched in the mirror as my Uncle Don look-alike nodded a deadpan agreement about this fantastic haircut. The person I had known... well, for-ever, was no longer looking back at me.

I had to get out of there. I quickly paid and nearly ran to Val's car. As soon as I got in the passenger seat, I lost it.

"I hate it." I sobbed. "I hate it. I hate the way I look."

"You look great with short hair. It looks really good," she tried to convince me.

"It looks horrible. I look like my Uncle Don."

"No, you don't." She was trying to make me feel better and I would have none of it.

"I do."

"It really doesn't look bad, Michele. It looks kind of cute on you. It's just different. You'll get used to it."

"I won't have to." I was inconsolable. I was hysterical. "It's just that... it makes it real." I sobbed even harder.

"I know," she said. "I know Michele. It going to be okay."

Val decided to get her haircut after I scheduled mine, so we drove to a different salon that could fit her in that day. The solidarity haircut thing was endearing when we set it up, but now that I didn't recognize myself, I only wanted to hide until I could rediscover me. I tried to pull myself together on the way. I took a few deep breathes. I wiped my eyes and took a few more. *It's just hair.* I told myself.

I avoided eye contact with everyone as we walked into the salon and slumped into the seat of a hair dryer like a surly teen-ager. Val's hair is super curly. Ten inches of length curled up into springs that barely reached her shoulders. The new cut would put those curls right close to her head. She'd look to me every now and then with her fair complexion and rounded cheeks and smiled gently. I avoided looking in any mirror, instead focused on how hard she was trying to make the most of this and forced a smile back. I counted the seconds until I could leave.

After her cut, Val dropped me off at my office. I immediately called Autumn, sobbing again as I recapped my uncle's hair and lost identity on the dreaded, steady march towards chemo. The scarf party was in an hour. I was a wreck.

She just listened, and then said, "Well, this is the first time I've heard you upset since this all started. So that's good." This was the clinical evaluation of my situation. Autumn works in behavioral health. The emotional processing of great strife was her forte. Next, she said, "Options...." This is another gift of Autumn's. She is so pragmatic in breaking down basic realities with empathy for the bigger meanings around them. "You don't have to go to the scarf party."

I hadn't even considered this. It took me by surprise. "But it's my party."

"You still don't have to go if you're not up to it," she said simply. "Or you could go, and we could skip the scarf part of the party."

"But that's the whole point. That's what people are coming for."

"Michele, we're doing this for you. To help you. If having the scarf party doesn't help you, we don't have to do it."

"So, everyone comes with scarves, and they sit there on the table, and we do nothing with them?"

"Yes, that's exactly what we'd do if that's better for you."

"What we would tell them? That I'm kind of a disaster right now and can't handle it?" I didn't know how to navigate this. I did *not* want to lose it in front of these people in a public place, or anywhere. It's just not how I roll.

"No, we'd just say, 'Thank you for the scarves, I'm going to try them on later' and then we'd just hang out."

I considered this. Autumn waited while I did.

"So, we could cancel the scarf party," I said. Would Autumn be able to get in touch with all of them in time? Would I just be a no-show?"

"Yep, you could skip it. I could go to let them know that you couldn't make it."

"Mm hmm." Not ideal, but it would get me out of it. I pictured them sticking around for a beer in my absence, talking about me. I didn't like that. "Or I could just go to it."

"You could." There was no recommendation in the way she said this. Autumn was giving me time to think.

"I don't want to go through all this again with them. I don't want to talk about my haircut."

"Then we won't." I could still go, and I did have options. Of all the things that were out of my control right now, this was not one of them. It felt good to be in control of something. This was my cancer, and I got to decide how I navigated it.

"I think I'll go to the party."

"Okay," said Autumn.

"I'm going to put a hat on."

"Okay," said Autumn.

"I don't know if I want to try on all the scarves. I think I'll decide when I get there."

"I'll come pick you up in 20 minutes."

In a hat, I could ignore the way I looked and feel like me. When Autumn picked me up, she ignored the hat and the hair cut it hid.

I intended that night to be light and fun, but I couldn't see now how it possibly could be. I thought of the women who would be there that night. My friend Sarah would be there, who always impressed me with her perspective. I remembered talking with her once about her ex. I asked her if it was awkward to share time with him in such a small town. She looked serious and thought for a minute before saying casually, "Everyone has their shit," and shrugged a *Might as well move on.* I thought of my friend Jen who would be there and felt the joy she always exudes in a natural and real way, her smile and ready laughter a balm.

Some of these women I hung out with regularly, but others only occasionally. With each of them, I'd had moments of deep connection, sometimes talking about the moments that shape our lives: the ones we expected, the ones that surprised us. Other times we'd sit with the quieter talk of hard times and how we got through them. With each of these women, individually, I'd shared a glass of wine or a beer while pouring over our histories and how they made us uniquely ourselves. As I walked into the brewpub that night, I realized immediately that we had shared our more delicate truths and the experiences that shaped us long after they had happened. After we had years to reflect on and process the events that shaped our views and perspectives. We would talk, back then, as people who had already recovered and felt grounded in who we were and who we wanted to be despite or with gratitude for whatever life threw at us. It was after our intimacies had long since scabbed over and healed into faint scars that we would recount them, not while we were in in the middle of hard times.

With each step I took towards the party, I felt exposed in the middle of a gaping wound, in the raw, sensitive stickiness of it, the deepest hurt I'd ever experienced. It was a gash too sensitive to fit a crowd.

Also, I was the common thread that brought the lot of us together that night. Some of them would be meeting for the first time. My imminent hair loss was the star attraction, and with as fragile as I still felt, I had no idea how I'd keep the conversation rolling with all eyes on me. The Michele with cancer was a complete stranger. I might not be able to get it together if I started to crumble. If I felt it coming, I'd run fast and far.

I *knew* I did not want that. I walked up the balcony to my party intent on setting the vibe. If I was pitiful, everyone would respond to me with hugs and furrowed brows. If I acted like I didn't care, everyone would follow suit. I decided to put on a little "Fake it 'till you make it." *I'll just pretend I'm the me from before.*

Most of my ladies were already there. We crowded in a jumble of hellos and hugs and *How's it going?* Val walked up behind me then, and as I turned to greet her, she looked right at my hat, smiling and laughed a little, "You're gonna have to take the hat off some time."

Autumn butted in abruptly. She opened her eyes a little wider and looked right at Val as she said, "No, she doesn't have to take the hat off." A little aggressive, absolute.

"Come on, your haircut looks fine. And you're going to have to take it off to try the scarves on," Val kept working on making me okay with it.

"No, she doesn't have to." Autumn stretching her tiny little frame a few inches taller, stepped closer to Val, crow-winging her. Autumn made clear that this conversation was over. I tried not to laugh. Autumn, you feisty, little thing.

Their interaction made me see things more clearly. I didn't like the way I looked. And I didn't like that I had cancer. I could get hung up on how much I hated it. But the reality was that all of this was happening. It just was. But I was in control of how

I reacted to it. I could leave the hat on or take it off. I could sit slunched over all night and wallow. Or I could sit up straight and get on with it.

I've always found that honesty, and by that, I mean, honesty with the moment, absolute honesty to myself, to be exceptionally comforting. Even when, and especially when, there's something difficult to deal with. It helps me to just state what is, without judgement of my own feelings or anything else. It's almost as if I don't commit to truth, in all its complexities, the little voice in my head will start screaming all the things I didn't say. And then all those negative feelings stick with me.

"Well," I started, trying to stay steady and light, "I don't like the haircut. I mean I've had the same look for so long that it's hard to get used to. You know? And I don't like the reason I got it. But some hair is better than no hair, for now. I mean baldness is coming, right?." I shrugged. I repeated some version of that a few times to let it catch. Autumn stayed beside me to change the subject quickly each time. Before I knew it, we were talking about the day, about *non*-cancer things. We slipped right into the easy banter among women that I find so lifting. That they didn't know each other didn't matter. That I had a horrible freaking haircut didn't matter. That I had cancer even didn't matter. What mattered was that people who care about me showed up to give me a little love. That is no small thing. The beauty of it filled me, and I started to remember that I was more than just cancer.

We gathered around the table, and I decided to start opening packages. The first one held two scarves. The first was a long, rectangular red scarf, covered with silver spots. Its mate was of the same style but in green.

"Those were my grandmother's," said my friend Abby.

"They're beautiful." I told her, letting the sheer fabric slip through my fingers. "Well let's try them out." I took a deeper breath, slowly so no one would notice, and took my hat off, steeling myself to ignore my hair. I wrapped the red one around my head and tied it gently at the base of my neck. I looked to my crew and raised my eyebrows. "What do you think?"

"I like it."

"It's the color."

"Yeah and that will go with anything."

"There's this green one too," I showed them. I looked at Autumn, thinking *We're doing this.*

"The color is even nicer on that one," she smiled. *We're right here for you.*

"I love it," I smiled back at her. *Thank you, A.*

We spent a couple hours opening scarves and testing them out. I'd model each one so that my women could tell me how much they loved them. We played around with how to tie the larger square scarves. We tried a double wrap on the longer ones. We talked about what I could wear with each one. We noted that the smaller ones might come in handy sometimes. The scarf party was *fun.*

For me, that party came with a big realization about how substantially I would influence my experience while I'm in the middle of it. That I could navigate cancer in my way. That cancer doesn't take away who I am. By letting people in around the edges of this wound, if not the center of it, I invited their love and support within my experience. If I stay alone in the center of hurt, I miss that. I didn't want to miss that. I decided to take my cancer on with this attitude. And I would need to be reminded of it shortly after the scarf party, when the real hair loss began.

Welcome Distractions

I put on my blog persona of upbeat cancer fighter to send out a post just before my first chemo infusion. Without intention, there became a recipe for my posts: keep it real, if slightly sugar-coated, without getting into uncomfortable details. No fluids or body functions mentioned. I sprinkled in some humor as I laid out treatment steps and opened windows (not doors) to my feelings about them. I was guiding the communal approach to cancering. *We're looking this thing directly in the eye. We're not scared to use its funny sounding words. We'll state them, without wavering, because there is no pity here.*

Posted by Michele, December 6, 2011

> *… Everyone reacts differently to chemo and researching all the possible side effects can really bum a girl out. So, I'll just wait and see how it goes for me. And if it really sucks, then hey, Wednesday is one down and only five to go.*

By the time I was scheduled for my first infusion, I'd had multiple explanations of process. I knew what to expect in concept. But when I imagined myself as the chemo recipient, I felt completely unprepared. Since the chemo would be rough on my veins, and chemo leaking outside your veins is really, really bad, I opted for a port. A port is like an implanted artificial vein. It provides easy access to pull blood out and to deliver meds in like an IV. A week after my second surgery, I was back at the hospital in Duluth for another round of anesthesia to install the port. They cut a slit in my chest to slip the port in there. It was a thin disk maybe an inch in diameter connected to a tube that lay under my skin and ran up to and over my collar bone. I remember the casualness with which the surgeon told me she was going to cut into my jugular vein and insert that tube into it. I thought instantly of *National Geographic* movies where lions go for the quick kill via the jugular. The jugular! The vein that could let blood flow like a fire hydrant. Can you imagine the first doctor that thought this up? *I have an idea. Let's cut open the jugular. On purpose.* With a direct route to my heart, the port would allow the chemo to mix with my bloodstream throughout my body.

I knew a needle was going to be inserted, eased in I figured, into that port in my chest. As the nurse leaned over me, pushing on the edges of the port to find its rubber center, a spike to the chest started to seem way more intrusive than a friendly poke in the arm.

When I was sufficiently sterilized and sprayed with a light pain killer, she grabbed a fat, inch-long needle set perpendicular to a square piece of plastic. She hovered that needle over my chest and said, "Take a breath." I drew in as much air as I could, hardly any intake at all, because I was hypnotized by that needle actively growing. She prompted me further, "Take a deep breath." When my chest rose outward with the pressure of full lungs, she abruptly rammed that needle all the way into me, the flat plastic now resting flat against my skin. I felt my eyes open wide as I uttered an astounded, prolonged, "Wow." I didn't dare move for the entire two-hour infusion.

I kept waiting for something to happen, for the mic to drop and all the side effects to kick in at once. But they didn't. I felt so unaffected I stopped by my office that afternoon. I even took the stairs. There was a handful of board and staff members gathered in the entryway. They froze when I entered and looked at me for signs of - something. I threw my hands up with a shrug and said, "I don't know! I feel fine?" We all were incredulous. One of them asked if I felt that needle in my chest. Nope. Another asked if I could feel the chemo dripping into me. Nope. It was the strangest thing.

Bob was there preparing for another drive down to Madison with a volunteer, a replacement for me, to argue against the mining legislation. I wasn't in the middle anymore. I didn't know what changes had been made to the bill, which legislators were the ones to talk to, which points we thought we had the greatest chance of influencing, what propaganda the backers of the legislation were promoting. I knew all that I no longer knew. I considered joining them to discuss the newest proposals. For a second. But I didn't. This was theirs to take charge of now.

Instead, I went back to my office and tried to find something to do with myself. I scrolled through some of my emails, but I all I could think of was the chemo coursing through my veins. I had no mental energy for work that afternoon.

I left the office and made it home by early evening, thankful that the girls had no knowledge of the big event. To them it was just another day, and I was so grateful for their cheerful distraction. My dad and his wife Pam were there to help. Just like my mom, they were anxious to come out as soon as they heard the news. My parents divorced when I was in second grade. We lived in Chicago at the time. My mom and dad's parents both lived in Pittsburgh, and a branch of the company my dad worked for had an office there as well, so we all moved back to Pittsburgh after their divorce.

My sister Heather and I lived with my mom in the suburbs after the divorce. We visited my dad every other weekend at his place in the city, just twenty minutes away. My dad married Pam when Heather and I were in high school and moved to a beautiful, unique house in the trendiest neighborhood in Pittsburgh. With Pam's impeccable taste, they remodeled the worn looking home into an elegant statement that could be featured on the cover of any upscale magazine. I found it fascinating, and unbelievable, that anyone's home could be so perfect all the time, even if you stopped by unannounced. When Heather and I became teenagers, we spent fewer full weekends there but visited often for scheduled dinners. Dinners were always formal affairs at Dad and Pam's place.

Discussion over dinner was an equally formal event, lasting hours mulling over big, important events. My dad has a passion for history and politics and is eager to dissect any opinion from all angles. When I'd tell him about any of my plans, he'd relentlessly hammer me with every possible hurdle that could trip me up. I'd never bring up any new idea until I thought I could anticipate everything I'd need to clear. At the time, those interrogations were a drag. All I really wanted was the support of *What a fantastic idea! Tell me about all this fun.* But I see now how working to exhaust all his questions with well-reasoned, well-presented answers, has largely shaped my approach to making big decisions. I like to be prepared.

When I moved away from Pittsburgh, visits were usually filled with well-arranged activities. But there was no time for a well-planned visit with cancer. And for the first time I felt no guilt in my lack of preparation. What's for dinner? I don't know. What's the plan for today? No idea. Since we hadn't spent much time in the comfortable silence that comes with living together, the free time in an unplanned visit felt notable.

We awaited the side effects after my first round of chemo. Pam was trying to anticipate every need by cooking and cleaning and making conversation. My Dad and I were speechless and foggy, still unable to believe that I had cancer.

"A package was delivered for you today. It's over by the couch," Dad told me. It was from a friend from Madison whom I'd worked with regularly over the years. I first saw the card. It was signed from my friend and a handful of other colleagues from down state. *Something to make you feel pretty,* it said.

I pulled back layers of tissue paper to uncover a stack of treasures. There were dozens of earrings: danglers and posts, some bright colors and others in simple silver designs. There were twisted paper necklaces from Africa and chokers with bold, colorful amulets. There were bracelets with charms; others made from strings of stone beads. There were brightly colored scarves with dramatic patterns in silky fabrics. Other scarves were simple, soft and cozy as lambs' wool.

With the girls on either side of me, we admired each piece as we tried them on as singles and in combination. I had forgotten that I told my friend that I didn't think being bald was going to make me feel super-hot. But she heard me and rallied her friends and family to raid their jewelry boxes. I hardly knew these people, yet they took the time to send love in silver, stone, fabric, and paper. It held such meaning, their selfless offering to help me still feel beautiful, despite the appearance I couldn't escape.

"This makes me want to be a better person," I told Dad.

Compassion in Community

I knew very little about the benefit, just that Jon's coworkers were planning one for me. Benefits are a standard here in northern Wisconsin. Maybe because of the close-knit nature of small towns, or maybe because there's a deeper empathy for the financial toll of illness when you live in an economically depressed area. Here, when someone gets sick, a benefit is organized almost instantly both to help financially and to make sure the person who's sick knows they are not alone. Jon and his coworkers would occasionally give me an update about my benefit: who was providing food, the donated raffle items, the band, etc. They brushed it off as easy, seamless, nothing but a pleasure to plan.

On a Saturday afternoon, just three days after my first infusion, Jon and I drove to the local bar, Four Corners, listening to the girls' banter and giggle in the back seat. I peeked into the side mirror. "Make sure Dad and Pam are still behind us." I sat back in my seat then and said, "Well I'm glad I'm able to go."

He glanced over to ask, "How are you feeling?"

I shrugged. "Pretty okay actually. Just a little of everything. A little nauseous. A little tired." I looked out the window at the fields of hay. "A little nervous."

"Why are you nervous, Mama?" asked Lil from the back seat.

"Oh, you know how it feels sometimes when you're going to a party. Just getting ready to see our friends."

"Skyler is going to be there, Mama. She said so at school yesterday," Caitlin exclaimed.

"And my friend Rallie. She's coming with her whole family. She told me," chimed in Lil. They were more focused on the excitement of their school friends coming to the benefit than the reason for it. I was relieved that the no-need-to-worry-about-Mom mode was still intact.

"Is it going to be a big party Mama?" asked Caitie Ray.

"I don't know honey. I guess we'll just have to wait and see when we get there."

Jon looked over at me and said, "I think it's going to be huge, Michele."

I thought about that for a minute. About being in the center of my cancer party. "No speeches." I told him.

"I know, I told them that. No speeches."

One day last week, the thoughtless comments of a stranger during one short shopping trip shifted my feelings about the benefit from excitement to apprehension. Caitlin and I went into town to get new mittens. I held her hand as we walked down Main Street, until she saw one of the posters announcing my benefit taped up on a storefront window.

"Hey Mama Look! It's a picture of us," said Caitie Ray. "Let me see it!" I picked her up so that we could study the poster together.

It was printed on a legal sized piece of paper, framed in the color of breast cancer with a series of twisted ribbons lining one side. A picture of the girls and I from a vacation last summer at Niagara Falls filled the top half. They were leaning into me with the tired look that comes with posing for too many family pictures on vacation. We all look frumpy, hunched over, and travel worn. It seemed to fit its purpose well. We leaned forward to read the brief blurb about the benefit.

Help our community "Stand Behind Michele" at a potluck benefit for Michele Wheeler, who has been diagnosed with breast cancer, Donations and proceeds will help the family pay for Michele's surgeries and treatments.

I had seen the poster a million times by now. It was posted up at every business in town. I saw it attached to the stand at the checkout line in the grocery store. I'd pass it ten times if I walked two blocks. I was all around me. As I held Caitlin up to study it, I wondered, worried, what she saw in it. Best not study it too long.

"The party is going to be a lot of fun." I told her as I put her down and held her hand again. She pointed out every poster the rest of the walk to the store.

"Mama, there's another one!" exclaimed Caitlin.

"Yep, there we are kiddo,"

"Mama, you are everywhere."

I smiled at her. "That's so nice, huh? Dad's co-workers put those up for us."

"Are you famous?"

"Not famous. Let's get you some gloves in here." I glanced at the poster by the door on our way in.

We found Caitlin a pair of warm gloves and brought them up to the counter. I felt Caitlin leaning into me, just barely able to see over the counter. An older woman I didn't know picked up the gloves up and scanned them. When I handed her my card, I could feel her studying me for a moment. Then she asked, "Is that you on the poster in the window?"

I looked back at her, startled. "Ummm... Yeah. That is me."

"Well what's the matter with you?"

Caught off guard, I stared at her for a moment and then said flatly, "I have breast cancer."

"Oh. Breast cancer. It's everywhere." She rolled her eyes and swiped the air with her hand. "My neighbor has breast cancer, and she is just having a horrible time with the chemo." She gave me a quick once over, "You look fine but, she was *really, really* sick for months. My sister had breast cancer too. She made it five years before it came back, came back hard." I stood there speechless and paralyzed. "She only lasted another year or so. Died three years ago. In the end, she was just so *tired* of being *tired*. Don't get me wrong, she put up a good fight. I'll tell you that." With that I felt Caitlin beside me stand a little taller to see above the counter. I was so shocked I couldn't find words. "My uncle had prostate cancer. Now that's an aggressive one. He only made it a few years before he died...."

I felt a tug on my hand and looked down to Caitlin. "Mama... Mama, are you going to die?" she asked me. Her voice trembling, big fat tears just about to spill from her eyes. She was terrified.

And with that, my shock turned to red hot rage. It coursed through every bit of me like the roar of Niagara Falls at flood stage. I leaned over slowly and held Caitlin's shoulders gently. I turned all of that rage into conviction, forced myself to soften my voice, to not look angry and definitely to not look scared as I said, "No, honey. I am not going to die. Every cancer is different. And those cancers she's talking about are not like the one I have. It's not that way for me."

She looked right back at me with her eyes wide, deciding if she could believe me. I tucked her hair behind her ear. "I am not...I am *not* going to die."

She nodded slightly. I gave her a small smile before turning back to the cashier. Without looking at her, I said, "Give me my card back." She started to say something else, and I put my hand up. "Just stop. Give me the card and just stop." I signed the receipt and contained my rage again as I reached for Caitlin's hand gently. Neither of us spoke as we walked back towards the car staring at the sidewalk. I saw her glance up at the posters along the way. They looked different to her now.

I shook her hand slightly then, "You know what I think we should do?" She didn't look at me. "I think we should get ice cream."

She hesitated a minute and said softly, "I think we should go home, Mama."

This kid never passed up ice cream. But it would mean another store, and another poster. She was right. We should skip that. "I think we have some ice cream at home. Let's go home and sit by the fire and have a great big bowl of ice cream." Eyes still fixed on the sidewalk, she nodded slightly. I tugged on her hand playfully and said, "Let's have one bowl so big we can share it, huh?" Another nod. No eye contact. I loathed that woman at the store.

I recapped the store experience in separate accounts to Jon and Autumn later that night. Jon listened quietly as I railed against the store clerk. I'd repeat just a few of her words before I had to stop and close my eyes, then shake my head. Each time I thought of Caitlin hearing it all I'd feel a panicked terror of sadness and fury. He let me recount it a few times, eventually offering the woman a generous assessment, "People try to relate to each other by drawing from their own experiences. And unfortunately, with cancer, many of those experiences don't have happy endings. She was trying to relate to you in the only way she knew how. She just didn't get it right."

I knew he was right, but I couldn't get there. I'd get a half step into empathy for her but would quickly be filled with rage again. *How about you have a little empathy towards me, you know, the one with cancer? How about you think—for just one second—about my child standing next to me?*

Autumn gave me more of what I wanted. A conversation full of *Are you freaking kidding me? How could she...*

"I couldn't stop her," I told Autumn. "I could feel my mouth hanging open, just stunned."

"What the hell! How's Caitlin doing?"

"I think she might hold on to that for a while." I shook my head and took a deep breath, wishing I could erase it, knowing I couldn't. "I won't ever let that happen again. I can't let someone else direct the cancer conversation to places I don't want it to go. And I guess I'm just not going to leave the house unless I'm emotionally ready to do that."

I could feel, too, that the disaster at the store was starting to influence my feelings about the benefit. I knew it shouldn't. I didn't want it to, but it was. Would I have the energy, chemo side effects still unknown, to pre-emptively control the narrative with everyone there? The intensity of all that attention, and managing it, was starting to terrify me.

"Will I have to get up and like, address the crowd?" I asked her.

"Not if you don't want to," she assured me. I grinned, imagining her snuffing out any calls for a speech immediately.

"But what if it just ends up happening," I sighed, "and I'm surrounded by all these people staring at me waiting for - something?"

I wished I had the composure and elegance to speak to everyone. To tell them how incredibly moved and appreciative I was. To have the composure to let them know what a lift it was that they showed up. But the emotion of it was too much. Too much love, too much cancer. Too much intensity. I knew I couldn't do it. The thought of breaking down in front of a packed house made me feel fully panicked.

"What am I going to *say* to people?" I asked.

"Just tell them, 'thank you for coming,'" said Autumn simply.

I was replaying my conversation with Autumn in my head on the way to the benefit. Jon reached over and grabbed my hand, "We'll stay as long as you want."

I tried to settle myself down. "It'll be good. Once we get there it will be fun." We were about a half a mile away when I noticed a car parked on the side of the road far up ahead of us. "Oh, hey look. I think someone has a flat up there."

"Ahhh. Nope," Jon said slowly as we approached. "I think this is for you."

"What?" I sat up to get a better look. As we got closer, I saw that the car was the first in a very long line of vehicles. *Oh my...* We followed the cars up to Four Corners and saw that the line of cars continued down the road in every direction as far as I could see. Jon pulled into the spaces saved for us in the back. Dad and Pam pulled in behind us.

"There are *a lot* of vehicles here," my dad said as he got out of the car.

I nodded in response, just as shocked, and we headed in. As we walked around to the front door, we saw a friend leading a team of horses pulling a flat-bed trailer stacked with hay bales. A pile of kids and their parents erupted with shouts and laugher, calling our names and waving when they passed by.

"Mama, horses!" The girls started bouncing, waving wildly at their buddies. "Can we ride on the wagon?"

"I wanna ride on the wagon!"

I waved back to the trailer of friends and said, "You bet kid-dos. You'll get a turn." I looked at the smiles and excitement on my girls' faces and was so very thankful that Jon's co-workers had planned fun into the event. A *horse drawn wagon* screamed fun, not cancer.

Jon told them, "Let's go on in and then you can come back out for the next loop."

Four Corners was the gathering place for our disperse community; we were there regularly. The owner, Dave, creates an atmosphere that welcomes farmers, loggers, hippies, young and old equally. He has a fantastic laugh and eyes that crinkle deeply at the edges when he smiles. We walked up a broad set of wooden steps to the entrance, meeting more people who shouted hellos and raised their beer glasses to me along the way. I smiled and waved back. As Jon opened the door, the feeling and energy of the room poured out like water from a broken dam. It was absolutely packed in there.

I stepped in and saw Jon's coworkers, Rachel and Jessica, seated at a table with a money box and a pile of raffle tickets.

"Well hey there!" Rachel shouted over the band. "Glad you could make it."

I leaned across the table to hug her and said, "I'm glad to be here. I'm feeling pretty good actually. This is...." I looked back at the room, "... this is crazy!"

Jessica laughed, "People have been coming in non-stop for the last hour." I looked down and saw a large framed photograph of a close-up of a little drop in a stream lying on the table. The rocks and leaves on the edges were coppery shades of grey and brown with white frothy water rushing over the ledge. The picture was maybe eight by ten inches, but there was at least six inches of white matting all around it. "That's for you," said Jessica.

I leaned down to read the signatures written in varied handwriting and at random angles all throughout the white border. Lil walked up next to me. "What's that, Mama?"

"It's a picture for me."

"Why did they write on it though? You shouldn't write on a picture. I'd be in trouble if I wrote on it."

"Most pictures we don't write on," I said as I touched the frame. "But this one you can. Just on the white parts. It's a way to share this night, so I can bring a little bit of it home with me."

Lil read off some of the names, "'*Jason, Sarah and Sam.*' Is that red-haired Sam?"

It was Sarah from the scarf party, her husband, and daughter Sam. "Yep, that one."

"Oh! I know her! This one says 'We love you! Oh, that's nice Mama. Look at this one." She pointed to a skeleton of a little tree with Love ya lady! scrawled underneath its branches.

"Valena wrote that one." I told Lil. The girls loved Valena. She was a good friend who they embraced as "Auntie Viva." She often made time to spoil the girls with her love and attention.

"Viva's here? Caitlin! Viva is here."

I wanted to sit and read each name scratched in sharpie, over and over, overwhelmed by the connections I felt with every signature. I looked back to Jessica and Rachel, "This is beautiful," I said, seeing more of how much they put into this benefit for me. "Thank you. For all of this."

"Oh, Diane brought the picture for you," said Jessica. "And the rest of it was no problem." She waved off planning a party for a few hundred like it was nothing.

Just then Autumn's son, Caleb, burst out of the crowd and nearly tackled the girls with a hug, "Hi buddies!" Caleb exudes happiness. He is a bundle of energy and joy. It's impossible not to smile when you're around that boy. I adore him.

"Hey T-bub." I leaned over to hug him, using the nickname the girls gave him before they could pronounce his name. "Good to see you, big man."

He pulled back with uncontainable excitement. "Michele! You are having a really big party! Everyone is here." He rattled off names of their classmates.

"Where are they?" asked Caitlin, even more excited now. It was becoming a party for us all, not just for me. "Mama can we go find them?"

"Yeah, go ahead. Just stay inside, okay." And the three of them disappeared into the crowd.

I gave one last smile to Jessica and Rachel and turned to see Val sitting at the bar. "Hey! You made it!" she hollered over the talk and music. She hopped off her stool to hug me.

"I did make it," I said hugging her back. "When did you get here?"

"About an hour ago. They roasted the pig for pulled pork sandwiches and people brought about a billion side dishes. Are you hungry?"

"I... don't know...." I was too overwhelmed to even think about eating.

Val smiled. "You're feeling okay enough to be here?"

"I am." I said, realizing how okay I actually felt.

"I'm so glad you could be here, Michele. Everyone has been thinking so much about you." I just nodded and worked to find something to say to distract me from crying.

"This is awesome! Thank you for being here, Val." I hugged her again, and in that moment, I loved her a little bit more. I made my way down the bar hugging my friends in turn - *Thanks so much for coming*. We talked about the food, about the people, the bar, the weather. I glanced to my right and saw my neighbors, the stoic farmers. More hugs. *Thanks for coming!* I saw town board leaders that I worked with, mine supporters. *Thanks for coming!* I saw people who only weeks before were shouting my inadequacies in fighting the mine, but now they treated me just as a human. *Thanks for coming!* People were here from every sphere of my life. It was absolutely incredible.

I glanced around to see if Jon, my dad, and Pam were still with me, but I had lost them in the crowd. The space that normally held the pool tables was transformed into a loaded display of auction items: a keg of homebrew, a bold necklace of Lake Superior stones, a quilted jacket, maple syrup, a sightseeing flight in a local pilot's private plane. I found my dad and Pam on the other side of the auction tables but couldn't get to them with all the stops to say hi to another group of friends, and then another. With each greeting I settled into the rhythm of the evening a little more.

I saw Autumn across the room then. She looked my way and lifted her eyebrows at me. *Doing okay?* I smiled back at her. *All good.* The kids were with her, and she gestured to the food line to let me know she was getting food for them. I nodded.

I realized that I had it all wrong about the benefit. I was worried about cancer draping itself over every space, every word, leaving me to apologize for the unwanted guest I brought. Instead, the energy of all these people—friends and family, neighbors and coworkers—overwhelmed cancer and denounced it to a small spot in the corner.

At the next group of friends, my *Thanks for coming!* was no longer an escape. It now wrapped me up in the support and love from the hundreds of people who came to give, with no expectations. All my apprehensions dissolved. These were my people. As I walked around my cancer party, it felt more like a really big wedding. Cancer was there. It brought us all together that day, but as a community, we had come together more strongly than it. Cancer didn't hold title as the main event.

I spent the next three hours in short, happy conversations with everyone I knew in northern Wisconsin. I heard a lot of "You look great!" and joked in return that I was feeling so good that I considered trying to look more sick so that people wouldn't think I was making this whole thing up. The girls ran by me occasionally with a joyful gaggle of friends. It was nearing evening, but the party was showing no signs of slowing down. The silent raffle had come to a close, and there was a flurry of activity at the front table as people brought up their items and paid for them.

There were a few items that didn't have bids on them yet, so an ad hoc live auction started up. In random pairs, people started outbidding each other on the remaining items. I watched as a couple people started bidding up a plate of homemade cookies, until one finally yielded and the crowd cheered and laughed, raising a glass to a fifty-dollar plate of cookies.

Jon walked up and put his arm around me. "How ya feeling?"

I leaned into him. "I'm really, really good."

Just then we heard Rachel shouting from the front door loud enough to make it over the bar noise, "Alright everyone! We're going to give away the door prize now! Four tickets to see the Packers at Lambeau!"

"Holy shit. They got Packer tickets?" I said to Jon just as the girls ran up beside us. "Hey you two. Having fun?"

"I ate brownies," said Lily, remnants of it all over her face.

"I see that," I smiled at her.

Rachel continued, "Grab your tickets! The last 5 numbers are…"

We heard an eruption of cheers from the far corner of the bar. One of the girls' classmates from school was jumping up and down. Lily cried, "Mama that's Rallie! She loves the Packers. Ooooh. I bet she is so excited." The crowd cheered again, and we joined them with big whoops and clapping.

The raffle was the last scheduled event. After that, some people settled into the bar for the evening. Others started grabbing their things to leave. It was then that I fully saw the event as a whole. I was struck by how many people came together from different worlds and different perspectives and rallied around the most basic element of humanity: compassion. And acting on that compassion with no expectation of anything in return. I saw that living in community means respecting each other just as we are. Before we are boss or employee, before we're Republican or Democrat, before we're mine supporters or fighters, before we're black or white or red or any shade of brown, before we're male or female, we're all just people. And we have much to offer each other through the common threads of our joys and pains, in our fears and hopes. I felt tightly woven into the fabric of us, wrapped up and held by it.

I saw my dad and Pam talking across the room. I hadn't been able to talk to them all day, and I wondered then what this day felt like to them. We never went to these kinds of events when I was growing up. Support was offered individually. Thinking of this through my dad's eyes, I felt an overwhelming sense of pride in our community. People often ask me why we live far up north in Wisconsin. Not because of the cold, and the bugs and the long winters, the remoteness. But this. *This* is why we live here. Because a whole pile of people came out to let me know that they are here for me, and that it's going to be okay. People who have little, give much.

Well You Can't Stop Now

S even reasons it's great to be bald.

1. You look like a badass when you're bald, and no one messes with a badass.
2. Think of all the money you'll save on shampoo.
3. You can finally get that head tattoo you've been dreaming about.
4. Bad hair day? You won't have one.
5. The bald eagle is a symbol of patriotism. You'll be like extra patriotic.
6. You can roll the window down all the way and not worry about messing up your hair. Convertible? Bring it!
7. You can rub your own head for good luck.

My sister Heather sent me that list of baldness perks. One of the many small gifts or notes she sent to make me laugh. We were mending our year's separation, without directly acknowledging it. Heather has always had a knack for taking something awful and making it smaller with humor. That woman is funny.

The switch to baldness was one of the chemotherapy side effects I dreaded the most. When my hair didn't fall out right away, I wondered if I would be one of the lucky few who did not experience hair loss. But then I wondered if hair persistence meant the chemo wasn't attacking fast-growing cells as well, which would mean it wasn't attacking my fast-growing cancer cells either. I told myself this was unfounded and unreasonable, but nearly everything that happened to me since I was diagnosed begged the question *What does this mean?*

It was about two weeks after my first chemo treatment, after my Dad and Pam went back home, that my hair started to go. The girls were coloring at the dining room table; Jon and I were in the kitchen prepping dinner. We had been talking about taking our house off the market. After three years with no little to no showings, we were considering taking a break. Like we needed more big change, or big decisions, right now anyway. We had been ignoring it. We were joking that we were now hoping it wouldn't sell when I pushed my hair back off my face without thinking about it. But when I brought my hand down, I saw a massive clump of hair in my hand. I was frozen in place when Jon turned and saw it too. We stood there staring at the pile of hair in my hand. Well-rooted hair is so highly revered. Think shampoo commercials with glorious locks flipped around to let all that hair flow and shimmer down across your shoulders. We love hair. It's gorgeous. But as soon as its not attached, when it's limp and dead, it seems horribly wrong. I didn't even want to hold it. We looked at my hair and then at each other for a second.

"I guess tonight's the night," I told him. He quietly looked back at me. "I don't know what to do with this," I told him quietly, looking at my hair. "Do I just throw it away?"

"Here, give it to me," Jon held his hand out. I waited while he thought for a minute, folding my hair into a manageable ball. He focused on it as he said, "Remember that grassy spot on our property in the opening in the woods where we had that picnic last summer? I'll go put it there. We're not putting any part of you in the trash."

I stood in the memory of that day for a moment, the time before all of this cancering. "Okay," I said. "Well, we might as well get rid of the rest of it then." I had already decided that when it would really start to go, I would take a shave. I called to the girls, "Hey you two."

"What Mama?" said Caitlin without looking up from her picture.

I put extra lightness in my voice. I assumed a *No big deal* attitude. "Remember how I said I was going to lose all of my hair?" They turned to look at me with big eyes and nodded. I had their full attention now. "I think it's time to shave this stuff off."

"Right now?" Lily looked at me with wide eyes, stuck between excitement and apprehension.

To prevent her from thinking anymore about it I kept moving. "Yep, right now," I turned off the stove. "Let's go up to the bathroom."

We brought a stool up from the kitchen and I perched myself on it facing the mirror. The girls crowded around me chattering while Jon plugged in the clippers.

"Are you really gonna shave it, Mama?" asked Caitlin. They do well when I keep on talking, so I kept it going.

"Yep, we're going to shave it off." If they see me upset, then they get upset. I buried all my dread and hatred of this moment and made myself as casual as I could. "The chemo works that way. So, when my hair falls out it's actually a good thing. It tells us that it's working to kill the cancer."

"But maybe your hair won't fall out," said Lily.

"I know! I was wondering the same thing," I reaffirmed her thoughts about it. "But when I was downstairs just now a bunch of it came out. So, I figured I'd just go ahead and shave it. I think it will be easier that way."

"But Momma, don't you want your hair?" asked Caitlin.

"I do," I nodded. "I would rather have it. But it's okay. It'll grow back." I swallowed the lump in my throat and shrugged a *whatever* shrug.

"Mama, you've always had your hair," Lily was quieter now.

"I have, honey," matching her quiet tone. I looked at her and smiled. "But it's kind of like when I got my short haircut. It was a big change, it was a little weird for a while, but we all got used to it."

Jon joined in the conversation, "Maybe Mom is gonna look really hard core. She's going to look tough!" He smiled at the girls, then softer he said to me, "Ready?"

I was not ready. But wanted to get it over with. I looked at the clippers in Jon's hand and felt the consuming stench of panic. I had to look away, so I turned to the girls, added a little fun to my voice to try and keep it light for them and said, "What do you think girls? Ready? Should we do it?" They were uncomfortable. They nodded little uncertain nods. I nodded back a big dramatic, resolute nod. "Okay then, let's do it."

With that, Jon lifted the clippers in front of my eyes and up past my forehead to shave a path from front to back. I put my face in my hands for a moment and ordered myself not to cry. Then I sat up straight again. I looked at him in the mirror and said, "Well you can't really stop now."

"A lot of hair came off in that one Momma!" Lil cried, hands over her mouth in astonishment.

"It sure did, kiddo," I said, determined to make head shaving fun.

"There it goes!" shrieked Caitlin, both of them giddy.

We weren't far in when the change in Mama's look was too much. Lily covered her eyes. She looked back up at me, "Oooooh...Mama!" and then hid her face again. "It's ugly Mama! It's so ugly!" She ran out of the bathroom.

"Hey..." Jon started to follow her. I put my hand on his arm to stop him.

"Let her go," I said. "Just finish."

Caitlin stayed in the bathroom until my hair was a fuzzy stubble about a quarter inch long. I shook the hairs from my shoulders and went to go find Lily. She was hiding under all the covers in her bed. I sat down next to her. Jon waited in the doorway.

"Hey kiddo," I started softly. She didn't move. I tried to coax her out from under her blankets. "Bug," This has been Lily's nickname since the moment she was born. She started cute as a bug and has remained so ever since. She was born with her eyes wide open, taking in the world. Observing everyone and seeing right through them. She's an old soul. She gets what's happening around her so completely. She is full of kindness and compassion. This is the kid whose lip would tremble at all the Disney movies, for the characters vilified as well as the heroes. She usually hides her feelings well, but today's emotions were too big to handle. This scared her. Lily is very much my daughter. There are times when I can tell what she's feeling just by looking at her. I saw all of her in the hidden heap of blankets.

I gave her a second and then said, "Hey Bug. Come on out, honey."

She peeked out and grimaced before quickly hiding her head again. "I don't like it, Mama. It's ugly!"

"Lil," I said softly. "Same Mama. Different look."

She peeked out and looked at me.

"Same Mama," I said again. "Different look." I said this with absolute certainty. Now fully believing it myself and willing her to feel the same. She stared at me, deciding whether or not to accept this.

"Guess what I realized though," I said this like it was the start of a secret, like the introduction to something irresistible.

"What?" She lowered the covers a little more.

"I realized that I have a very nicely shaped head," I told her. "Some people have a little pea sized head. Just a tiny little thing. Other people have a big old melon. But I think I'm well-proportioned over here."

"You're what?"

"I mean my head is the just the right size. I didn't realize that with all my hair in the way. And..." I hesitated to keep her playing along with me. "I think it's a nice oval shape. Not too skinny. Not too round. Yeah," I nodded my decision. "It's a nicely shaped head!" I touched my fuzz of hair. "It does look funny though doesn't it, to have the hair gone? It feels really funny. I kind of like it though. It's really soft. You should feel it." I leaned over. She hesitated. Then she reached out with one finger and touched it like a hot stove. "Doesn't it feel soft?" I asked her.

"It is kind of soft, Mama," she agreed.

"I like the way it feels actually." I stroked it a little more until Lily did the same.

Caitlin jumped on the bed to join us and said, "Oh! It's like a stuffed animal Mama." Caitlin has always had a sense for what people need. Instead of thinking over and around something, she just seems to absorb the emotions of other people and tries to make them feel better. She has her father's ready call to fun, and as a kid she was always more eager to jump right into things. She rubbed my head up vigorously and hung on me with smiles and laughter to deliver the *hair loss is fun* vibe I was striving for. "It's all fuzzy!"

"It sure is. My scalp hasn't seen daylight for so long. It's so white, isn't it? It's weird to feel that too." Jon waited in the doorway while the girls and I checked out my crew cut until it was no longer hard to look at. Until we were comfortable enough to let the scary part of it go.

Helping my girls get through that evening made me see the core of what's important: We are important, all of us together. The love we have for each other is important. My hair did not matter at all. Not one little bit. I knew this of course, but my girls helped me feel it with absolute certainty. And with them, I fully let it go. Making it so my girls would be okay, that was worth my energy. In trying to help them by being a strong mom, I felt more like one. It wasn't an option to be anything less. They bring out the best of me, and they continue to do so, without even knowing it.

Tango Interlude 1

There's a warmth to the night. A hint of the change in season. Summer is coming. The air is thick with the taste of it. Just a little longer, and it will be here. It feels like they are on the roof all the time now, deep in the movement of Tango. It has become second nature. She stares hard at the open sky as they strut across the dance floor. When it is time to turn, she turns her head abruptly with a sharp stop. It makes him smile. She started Tangoing this way three nights back, and now he looks for it at each turn. She grins slightly in acknowledgement that her new trait has been recognized, awaited. She takes a step back then, improvising, and twirls twice before coming back to him. *Didn't expect that though did you?* He almost laughs, but instead just catches her as she comes back to him. As soon as he does, the accordion cries its final stanza, leaving them standing face to face. For a second, they almost forgot what they were doing up here. For a second, it was just a dance.

They are caught staring into each other's eyes, catching their breath from the work of the night until a singular thought engulfs them. *I cannot freaking believe we are doing the Tango under the light of the moon.*

Hope for Me

After a couple rounds of chemo, I had a good sense of the pattern of side effects. The strength of the medicine peaked about three days out from an infusion. My routine was to get in a few days of work until I needed to spend a few days resting on the couch. After that I'd crawl out of exhaustion for the remainder of the three-week cycle. By the time I was on the upswing, it was time for another infusion, the starting point pulled back a few steps each round.

I sent out blog posts after each infusion to tick off the time and count down to the end. I posted to tackle all of the cancer talk in one fell swoop for family and friends near and far. It helped manage having cancer in a closely-knit, small town. I kept them light to keep us all light.

Posted by Michele, February 7. 2012

*It's becoming old hat by now. And ...[Chemo] went just
fine. Such a great group of people that work in the chemo
department in Ashland. Kind, kind people that amazingly
keep the space feeling fun.*

I was trucking along through treatments, counting them down.
It all became more commonplace, even having the needle
rammed into my chest.

But the cumulative effect of chemo was catching up with
me. I no longer had the mental energy for novels, so I switched
to magazine with more pictures than words. At my third infusion, I settled back into one of the big, cozy reclining chairs with
my newest addition of *Garden Designs* to pass the time. I had
reclined when a frail looking older woman reached the doorway.
I looked up and smiled as she shuffled slowly into the room.

"Good morning," I said.

"Morning," she replied, focused on getting her own self settled. She was so thin and petite. I wondered how she managed
her shoulder bag. It looked heavier than she did. She had the
classic older woman haircut: dyed a shade of medium brown
and permed into a well-sprayed football helmet. The wrinkles
around her eyes and mouth made her look like someone who
had spent a lot of time smiling, even at the moment she wasn't.
As she was getting settled into her chair, I put my magazine
aside and waited to see if she was interested in talking.

"Well it's warmed up a bit out there," she said looking over
to me with tired eyes behind thick, brown-rimmed glasses.

"It has," I agreed. "Nice to get past that cold spell."

"My husband dropped me off at the door. It's still too cold for me. I just can't keep warm."

"It's the wind," I commiserated. "Really pulls the heat out of you."

"Yes. He'll be here soon enough though," she said with the slow, thoughtful cadence of the elderly. We sat in silence for a moment. I was just about to pick up my magazine again when she asked, "So what kind do you have?"

"Breast cancer," I told her. "This is my third infusion though. So only a few more to go."

"That's not too bad. Has it been too rough on you?" she asked.

"Not so much," I said. "I spend a lot of time sleeping. But other than that, it's okay."

"Oh well that's fine," she said. "Are you from here?" In northern Wisconsin, you're only *from* here if your grandparents lived here. You might be able to get away with a racy statement like, "I'm from here" if your parents were born here. But that's still pretty questionable.

I told her we weren't, and asked, "Are you from Ashland?"

"I am," she said with pride. "Lived here all my life." There was a brief pause, then she said slowly, "Well there's no hope for me. I've got it all over and the treatments aren't working. We're keeping at it, but it's getting the better of me." I said nothing. I wanted to respond, but absolutely nothing came to mind. She continued, "There's nothing else they can do. I guess I only have just a couple months left."

Even though we were in a cancer center, I was blindsided. Her reality was the root of all cancer patients' fear from the first words of our diagnosis. I was entrenched in treatments, engulfed in a similar world, but I didn't realize until that moment that I had pushed the prospect of dying to the farthest reaches of possibility. To a place so remote there was nothing to see, and then I had turned all my attentions the other way. I didn't know how to talk about looking at death.

"I'm sorry to hear that," I finally managed, knowing how inadequate it was.

"My husband and I have been married for fifty years. We went to high school together. Oh, that was many years ago now." She looked straight ahead as if she was watching the memory, seeing the web of her life ahead of her, and the connections that would be broken when she was gone.

But then her expression changed as she returned to the present and she said, "He just gets so sad. When he thinks about it, you know? I told him, 'You're going to have to get someone to clean up around here.' I don't know how he'll get by."

"Fifty years is a long time."

She looked at me briefly then. "It is a long time." And then she looked away again, like the pain of time cut short was too much. "He doesn't do the cooking you see. Or the shopping. Never has. I don't even know if he could find the grocery store," she smiled at that. Her eyes were dry. I tried to keep mine that way as well by smiling back.

"It's my grandson that I'm most worried about. My daughter's son. He's only six and he just cries and cries. He says, 'I don't want you to go, Nanna.' I don't know what to say then. But they have these books now. They can record you reading them." She looked at me again with the wonder of this. "You just push a button and it records your voice. Isn't that something?"

The room started to dissolve around me as I was drawn into her grief. I offered, "It is something" so she'd know that I was hearing her.

"There's the whole book there," she continued, "the words and all, so you can record yourself. I've been reading his favorite ones. The ones I read him all the time. So that he'll have them when I'm gone."

I was astounded that I was talking with this stranger on the inside of her pain, but it didn't feel misplaced. It was so heavy and beautiful to share such an intimacy. All I could muster was, "I'm sure he'll really treasure those."

"Well I hope so. I don't know what else to do for him." Still no tears but she sighed with sorrow. "I feel so bad for him. For all of them. They're..." she trailed off and stared at the air in front of her.

An oncology nurse walked in then and greeted me briefly before turning to my neighbor with a smile, "I'm here to give your arm a little hug." As the nurse took my neighbor's blood pressure, I studied my magazine to give them as much privacy as a double occupancy room allows. A few minutes later, I heard the nurse say, "It's high."

"What's that?" replied my neighbor, still seemingly distracted by her own thoughts.

"Your blood pressure. It's pretty high." My neighbor shrugged slightly.

"Let's try again," said the nurse. But when it was high again, she said, "Let's let Dr. Lalich know and see what he thinks." She helped the old woman up from her chair, and they slowly hobbled out of the room, neither looking back.

Since the infusion schedule changed, I had the room to myself that round. When the nurse came back in to check on me, she was as cheerful as ever, and found simple things to talk about. I admired her for it. When things started to unravel for one patient, she somehow managed not to bring that energy to the next one. Mostly I sat looking at the chair the old woman had been sitting in, replaying our conversation over and over. I couldn't stop imaging her ache and sorrow around everything she'd miss. I tried the magazine again, only to have the garden pictures interrupted by images of a little boy crawling onto his grandmother's lap.

There was something in the way she talked about her cancer and her fate. I couldn't let go of it. It stuck to me like wet clothes.

By midmorning, my infusion was complete, and I headed to my office intending to work for the afternoon. I slowly made the assent up two flights of stairs to my office, still soaked in my talk with the old lady.

I walked in on a conversation between Jim, our board treasurer, and Sara, a volunteer accountant who was trying to help us make sense of our books. I completely forgot that I had planned to meet them.

"Well hey there!" said Jim. "Did you have your infusion today?" He leaned back in his chair, pushed his glasses up on to his nose and exclaimed, "Ya know, that stuff is poison!"

I smiled at our recurring joke, about how dose is the only difference between poison and medicine. "Hey Jim," I pulled out a chair to sit down. "Poisoning complete."

I settled in next to Sara, who was super smart and an experienced accountant. We were fortunate that she was willing to volunteer for us. She was focused intently on her laptop and tapping the mousepad repeatedly, shuffling around numbers in our budget.

Jim leaned forward then to get into it. "Okay, so here's the thing. Sara and I have been working on the financial statements for the next board meeting. Like I told them last time, I have no idea what's happening with the budget." I smiled at this. Jim was erratic like Doc in *Back to the Future*, minus the crazy hair and white lab coat. He had a much better handle on the budget then he let on. He slid a piece of paper with a table full of numbers across the table to me. "I made this report for all the open grants and used an algorithm to forecast our budget with updated expenses. Good news!" He stopped to smile broadly and spread his hands wide on either side of him to make his point with enthusiasm, "I think we can pay all the bills for at least four months!"

"That must be a new record," I said as I picked up the report, trying to muster some enthusiasm for a rare bit of security.

"Well that's in the accounting program. Sara's working on reconciling this with the bank statements." Jim was worked up that after years of struggling to develop a functioning accounting processes, our budget numbers were falling into place.

Sara handed me another paper with a table full of numbers. I stared at it but couldn't concentrate. I tried to talk myself in to caring as she talked through it. I could feel myself squinting in concentration when she finished that sheet and handed me another.

"That one's the balance sheet for the next board meeting," said Jim. "But if they ask me anything about that one, we're screwed! You know that reminds me, I was having breakfast with my brother this week—you know the rocket scientist." He started recounting some completely unrelated side tangent about orbit speeds and galaxy garbage (apparently there's an enormous amount of trash in space—it's notable). Sara looked at him first with confusion, then concern. I tried not to laugh. I learned quickly to wait these detours out when working with Jim. He was lightening the mood. He'd come back around.

When he hit a pause in his story, I turned to Sara and said, "So the balance sheet. Does this one show us how much cash we have on hand?" I pointed to two different reports and asked, "Why doesn't this number match that number?" She said something about encumbered funds and timing and other things I couldn't follow. Annoyed, I keep trying. "Wait, which one is the financial statement?" She talked through them again, and I still couldn't follow. After a few more rounds I went from annoyed to frustrated and snapped at her, "Look I just want to know how much money we have. Why is it so hard to tell me how much money we have?"

The room became still in an awkward silence. After a moment, Sara tried again to explain, even though I was now being an ass to a volunteer. Four months ago, I didn't need to fight such frustration. I saw this new layer of organizational growth as exciting. *Never thought I'd be here, let's do this thing*! But now I didn't want challenge. I didn't want to bend to unwanted demands. I was just so tired, and I didn't want it anymore.

I made an excuse to wrap up the meeting, clarity on financial statements unresolved, and offered a lame thank you to Sara. I escaped to my office and slouched into the chair behind my desk with my head in my hands - unable to think. I heard Jim at the door and lifted my head. He grinned, and slowly eased into the chair across from me. We sat in all the complexities of that interaction in silence: the roles we had before, how they've shifted, wondering if they'll shift back, and when. Then I said, "I don't know if I can do this Jim."

He stood up, leaned over to pat me on the shoulder, offered a slight grin of empathy and said, "It's okay." Then he left.

I sat for another few minutes staring at my desk and thinking of the old woman and her grandson. In an effort to distract myself, I took a deep breath to reset myself and opened my email. The first one was from Matt, who was helping to manage one of the programs I normally led. His message requested that I answer a list of questions he provided in sufficient detail,. He needed my responses by the end of the week.

Need.

It was a completely reasonable request. He was trying to help keep my program afloat while I was out. He even tried to take the thinking out of it by listing out questions to respond to. It was exactly the kind of efficiency that I encouraged as director four months ago.

But now, it infuriated me, the directive to meet his *need*. It wasn't a shift to entirely different values, but rather a shift in the importance among them. The old woman in the infusion center needed to prepare for her death. Needed to help her husband find a way to continue even when she was gone. Needed to find a way to keep a connection to her grandson, knowing, painfully, that the memory of a child would fade unfairly over time. She needed to define the legacy she'd leave, with only a few months to go. We had the most real conversation, two strangers sitting peacefully on the inside of an open wound. And it was for that conversation that I sat staring at an email etched in sharply pointed font across the harsh glow of my computer screen as a different person.

I called my coworker. I let him know he'd have to wait.

Heather

Well of course we finally got an offer on our house right when I was in the thick of treatments. It was horrible timing. The work of packing up our house and moving seemed impossible. But after three years without a single offer, we figured we had to take it. Besides, the plan all along was to trade in the privacy of our wooded forty acres for the convenience of in-town life. Life was going to be easier in Washburn.

Thankfully one of the places we were interested in in Washburn was still available: a beautiful, traditional home built in the early 1900s that was in the middle of town, with enough privacy to make the transition from country life to in-town life bearable. With its tall ceilings and worn wood floors, it had all the charm of an old home, and all the needs of an old home as well. The lathe and plaster walls were riddled with cracks, giving spiders plenty of hideouts. Half the windows didn't open. One of the upstairs bedrooms was completely missing a wall. But it was in our price range. For now, we just needed to make it comfortable enough to ride out the rest of my treatments. Weeks in advance, Val and Autumn helped me chip away at packing weeks in advance, but my biggest helper was my sister.

We'd been reconnecting since my cancer diagnosis. We didn't talk about the full year that we didn't speak at all. Not one phone call, not one email. Not a word. We didn't talk about the recurring issues that continually gnawed at our relationship, because we've tried, and we didn't know how to do it.

Instead, we stayed with easy, fun parts of us. Because we're so close in age, we're often mistaken for twins. We look more alike that my own twins do. We have the same tall forehead and the same light eyes—although hers are more green and mine more blue. We have the same light complexion, although I'm probably a little redder. We're about the same height, although she's more petite, and I more broad shouldered. For as much as we are similar physically, our personalities and inherent ways are so different.

Compared to my sister, I am "the quiet one," which is kind of like saying that a gorilla is quiet, compared to an elephant. Those who haven't met my sister can't picture me as less outspoken. But it is true. Compared to my sister I am a wallflower. I am like a patch of Black Eyed Susans, maybe even the ones with orange hues around the center. There's color there and some contrast. They're a notable flower, happy to stand on their sturdy little stems and take in the rest of the garden around them. My sister is a broad swath of dinner plate dahlias, massive striking flowers in a complete spectrum of wild, brilliant colors. The patch of them shared with a random assortment of those red-hot poker flowers—the ones that look they came right out of a Dr. Seuss book. Flowers that unpredictably burst into fireworks. Shimmery hummingbirds flit all around the garden of her in bright, impossible, animated colors. Does that sound a little over the top? Exactly.

We've held these roles—the quiet one and the animated one - since we were young kids. Heather is wild. As teenagers, she pushed outward to find the boundaries. I sat back and watched, learning through her experience to avoid the confrontations that defined the edges. She was always the popular one in school. A true extrovert, she is fed by being at the center of a big crowd. When we were in high school, she always invited me to tag along with her and her friends. She always included me. I always felt a little uncomfortable with them, unable to meet the expectations of Heather Ferry's little sister. I was clearly less entertaining. All the cool kids two grades up called me "Little Ferry" and welcomed me anyway, because Heather welcomed me.

Later, when we both were home from college for the summer, she still invited me to every party. On those summer evenings, hot and sticky with humidity, a group of us would blare jam bands like Rusted Root and drink beers, putting them down only to dance wildly when our favorite songs came on. Later, guitars would come out around the campfire. Heather's booming laugh and raspy cackle could be heard no matter where I was. As the soundtrack of the party reached its crescendo, my sister would often be heard bellowing, "Yippee Kai Yay, Motherfuckers!" and the rest of the party would whoop in willing embrace of this absurdity. We laugh hysterically every time we remember it. She shrugs with a little bit of embarrassment, but more so with an "Oh well, it was a really good time though, huh?" kind of attitude. Because it was.

These intervals of big fun would be interrupted by the occasional blow up between us, an underlying current that we never resolved. We walked a fine, sharp line between outstanding fun and seismic fury.

But then I got cancer. And it was so much bigger and more chaotic than everything that it shocked us both into parley. We talked cancer and distraction, avoiding all the unspoken under-currents of *I'm still really freaking angry.* Or *I'm sorry that I totally pulled away.* Or *I'm dreading the moment when you bring it up.* Or *I've missed you.* We didn't talk about our fight, instead she stayed big sister to me and helped me find laughter in the middle of something horrible the way that only Heather can. She helped me update my Mom and Dad regularly, so I didn't have to repeat the details as much. She listened when I talked but didn't ask for more.

When we set the closing date on our house for late February, Heather and I talked about her coming out for a visit to help with the move. It would be our first meeting since the big fight, and part of me was worried that we'd slip into trying to fix the problems that tore at us. I didn't have the energy for it. Over the past few months of our truce, we'd reconnected in the shared, lifelong experience of siblings that can't be found in any other relationship. There's no one that knows me in the same way, in the same context, like Heather does. And vice versa. That unique connection to my sister fills me with such warmth, gives me a sense of grounding that can't be found anywhere else. I wanted that place with her. I wanted to feel like Heather Ferry's little sister for just a bit.

I remembered a friend's mantra for me: *You have cancer girl, so you get it your way.* I called my sister and told her that I really did want her here, but also made it clear that there would be "no relationship mending" on this visit.

There was a brief pause. Then she softly and slowly said only, "Okay."

There was something liberating in establishing boundaries, so I was more excited than nervous when Heather flew out about a month later. We were only a week away from our closing date and were horribly unprepared. Heather quickly took on the role of director of the move: how many people were able to help and on which days, who was bringing trucks to move the big stuff, and who would take which load first. She orchestrated it all and made a big pot of chili to feed everyone as well. She coordinated a cleaning crew, so that I wouldn't get sick with my weakened immune system. While she worked frantically to orchestrate the move and packed the things that I didn't get to, she kept us all laughing until we were all convinced that moving was actually a really good time. It will all get done. It will all be just fine.

But she would slow down to make time for her nieces. The girls love their Aunt Heather. They are attracted to her like moths to light because they positively glow under her attention. She'd stop everything at their slightest interest, rest her chin on her hand and lean in to hear their fears about leaving their old school. She nodded with empathy and asked them for more. She listened, and then masterfully, subtly, guided the conversation to how great their new school was going to be. If cool Aunt Heather said so—and she's a teacher, so she knows things—then it will be that way.

The day of the move, we went back to the country house to do a final walkthrough. It was surreal walking around my place, empty and soon to be the home of someone else. It had the noisy echo of emptiness, so quiet and still without the energy of our family. As I walked up the stairs, I ran my hand along the smooth ironwood log that Jon cut from our property and made into a railing. I walked through the girls' bedrooms upstairs and saw them crouched in the closets during hide and seek. I left their rooms and saw the hallway transformed into a fort of cardboard boxes and blankets when it was too cold to play outside. I passed the upstairs bathroom where we shaved my head. From any window of the house, I could see one of the forts the girls built in the woods. I recapped them all to Heather. That one is Wintergreen Valley. The grass fort is over there. The Down Tree fort is over there by the pond. I wanted to tie us to every memory.

"I think that's all of it." I said to Heather, still wrapped in the memories of us in the house. But then I opened up the freezer, "Oh shit."

Heather came over and peered in to see it packed with food, "I'll get a box from the car." How could I have forgotten this? Heather came running in with the box, and we started throwing hunks of frozen whatever into it.

Heather grabbed a package from the bottom shelf, and when she saw what was hiding behind it exclaimed, "What in *the hell* is that?"

I looked back and saw a bunch of orange crusty legs sticking up out of a pile of black tar. "Uh oh... crawdads."

"What? Why?"

Trying to make it less gross, I said, "They taste really good actually."

"Don't even. What are they stuck in?"

"I think that's apple cider we boiled down into a thick paste." I said, grimacing at the black ooze all over the bottom of the freezer, and bits of crawdad and other random freezer crumbs all through it.

"And you just poured it on the bottom of the freezer?" She looked horrified.

"Um, I think the jar we had it in broke. Oh. Yep, there it is." I said as I slowly pulled half a pint jar out of the tar, wondering how long it had been there without us noticing. That's a little embarrassing. No making that less gross. I heard a car drive up the driveway then and saw the new owner out the window. "Uh oh, she's here."

Heather leaned in towards the freezer at the crawdad tar patty and poked at it, "What is that?"

Heather never went fishing with Grandpap. She wouldn't touch the fish, and *definitely* not a worm. I was now kind of enjoying myself when I said. "That's their eyes and the antenna."

"Stop! Stop right there!" She put a hand on her stomach and gagged a little. "I'm out. Are you kidding me? It's like they busted out of the foil but then got caught mid-escape in that goo. With the little claws cemented in there. No way."

"How am I going to get it out of here? It's like... frozen stuck."

"Try this," she handed me a plastic wedge she found in a drawer and said, "I'll distract her."

I started prying at the frozen cider tar, using the wedge to pull up the edges and push back the little crayfish legs that were sticking up out of it. It was slow going. Heather went to work keeping the new owner engaged in conversation, her extrovert traits coming in handy now that there was frozen crawdad tar to deal with. I started to silently laugh behind the freezer door and scraped more frantically. They started walking my way, and I gave Heather a look. *Not done! Not done!*

She abruptly turned to the window on the opposite wall and said loudly, "...the pond though! That is going to be great! Have you walked around much there? Over there?" She gestured away from the kitchen. I scraped the last of the big hunks of crawdad off the bottom of the freezer. There was still a bunch of brown sticky streaks from the cider on the bottom, but at least the crayfish legs were gone.

I closed the door abruptly just as the new owner walked up behind me. "Oh hi, just a little final clean up there. Just some, yeah, I think that's it." I turned to Heather and as soon as I looked at her, I thought "laughing fever." Laughing fever was a very serious condition, a fit of laughter that usually only consumed us when our Mom was really, really mad at us. She'd chase us up the stairs with a wooden spoon, threatening but never delivering a good beating, and we'd howl with laughter. I'm sorry Mom, that was incredibly rude. But that uncontrollable laughter was an ailment! Horribly contagious! Heather was starting to grin, and I knew I was about to lose it. We had to get out of there.

I blurted out, "Ahh... enjoy your home!" and grabbed my crawdad cider garbage bags to run out the door. We laughed the whole way to Washburn.

Later that evening, we replayed the crawdad incident to Jon, the girls, and the friends who were still helping us get settled into our new place. We embellished the story, let the telling of it take longer than the event itself. Heather and I talked over each other, now in a full recurrence of laughing fever, to complete the picture of it — crawdad legs and all.

Heather's flight left the next day. We sat in the kitchen over tea and coffee talking around our need to talk, until the awkward silence and forced small talk was too much. I'd made us both commit to no relationship mending on this visit, but the air was so thick with the need to I finally said, "Look Heather, I—I know we have things to work out, and I do want to work them out. I just—I just can't right now." I resolved myself further and said, "Let me get through treatments, and then we can talk later."

Heather leaned forward then and said, "or, we could not." Those four words were monumental, because they were the crux of the problems we'd had for years. I wondered what it would be like to move forward instead of getting stuck in the past. Wondered if I could open up more and not leave her guessing how I felt.

We sat quietly, holding our mugs, mulling over this possibility. And then, ladies and gentlemen, for the first time ever, we stopped right there and let that little step be enough for the day. It was only with something with consequences as big as cancer that we could see past the small irrelevancies that block what's important. So simple, so basic. What's important is love. Love that sees character and heart so that people can be themselves, despite our limitations. Love that places more emphasis on how we care for each other, not in the broad strokes of generalities, but in the fine details that make each of us uniquely ourselves. I sipped my coffee, so relieved at the small step towards breaking our patterns. I sat with my sister enjoying the stillness of the morning and thought, *Well, this is exciting*.

Bob

Weeks later, Bob and I drove down to the Namekagon River to go fishing. It was a clear, blue-sky day in the mid-seventies. There is something about that first warm day after a long northern winter. The gloriousness of it cannot be overstated, nor can it be appreciated unless you've been deprived of it for so long. It starts when the snow melts. *Look! It's the earth! Rock hard frozen, but you can actually see it!* And then, the giddiness of fresh air through an open window. We try not to get too excited about it, because this is the Midwest and we're very subdued, but also because a two-foot dump of snow in May is not entirely unheard of.

Nevertheless, Bob and I were celebrating warmth with music played loud enough to hear over the rush of wind through cracked windows. We lobbed carefree conversation back and forth. I was treatment-worn from the cumulative effects of five rounds of chemo but made content by the sun and good company.

After an hour's drive, Bob turned into a small gravel parking area by the river. We were the only ones there. Tall spruce and balsam fir towered above us swaying gently with the wind.

Bob opened the tailgate of his truck, and we sat on it to prep our rods. "What do you think we should use today?" I asked. Bob used to be a fly-fishing guide and knew this stretch of the Namekagon River well. He knew which insects were hatching now, the way they'd emerge from the river on route to becoming adults, and he knew how to mimic them with a fly on the end of a line. It was nice to be in the moment, one that wasn't about cancer, simply talking with a shared appreciation for fish and river.

When our rods were ready, I worked to get into my waders. I looked up to see Bob busying himself doing nothing, so he didn't seem like he was waiting for me.

"Alright. I'm all set," I said, hoping I didn't sound winded from the effort.

I followed him on a short path through thick evergreen woods, only brightening up again when we reached the river. The Namekagon and its floodplain created a wedge of openness armored on either side by spires of deep green conifers. We reached the river at a meandering side channel, a detour that departs from the river and then returns to it after only a few hundred feet. It was small in comparison to the main river, more shallow and with a lazier current, a more approachable entry. The water was stained brown from the decomposing leaves in the wetlands upstream. The dark water gave the Namekagon a broody feeling as it carved its way through the woods. Yet it was inviting.

"See that seam over there?" Bob pointed to a line between fast current and a slow eddy on the far end of the side channel.

A fish might take advantage of the slower moving water to conserve energy but would then slip into that faster water to eat the insects drifting with the current.

"Yeah, I like that," I said, starting to feel the working of the river.

"I'll take the bank on this side if you want to start there. Does that work?" He was giving me the better spot to fish, the same way my Grandpap had years ago.

I gingerly stepped into the river, searching for the bottom. I stepped knee-deep into the stream and felt the familiar pressure of cold water against the outside of my waders. I hesitated, paying attention for a leak. No wet spots. Always a treat.

The current was evenly swift across the channel. I shuffled through it slowly to get closer to my fishing spot and further from the bank. I drew my rod back, letting the current pull my line downstream, and then flung it forward, trying to lay the nymph as gently as I could on the surface of the water right at the top of that seam. But my fly landed shy of my target, so I tried again, drawing my rod forward and back a few times to let more line through and get further reach. It took me three more tries before the fly landed where I wanted it and another couple casts to get my fly to float naturally downstream. I was so engrossed in the process that everything else around me was forgotten. There was just this. Just me and the river, the backdrop of trees and the rod I held. And Grandpap, there in all of it. The subtleties of the current I was fishing became more apparent with each cast. I saw Bob then in my far periphery moving up the opposite bank. I nearly forgot he was even there.

"You're tending that line really well," he said. "You have a good sense of it."

Even as a grown woman, a compliment of my line tending still made me feel pretty darn proud of myself, thank you very much. I thought about saying that I've been told I have a professional cast, but instead I just grinned and tried to at least outwardly contain how pleased I was with myself.

I didn't pull any fish from that seam, so we moved on. With each step, I searched for solid footing amongst the slippery cobbles before pressing hard against the current. The weight of the water flowing against me felt so heavy, heavier than it should have. I trudged upstream while, again, Bob pretended he wasn't waiting for me, just indecisive about the next spot to fish.

We reached the mainstem of the Namekagon, wider than the side channel but still just knee deep. Bob gestured towards another seam between fast and slow currents and nodded to let me know I could take it. He started fishing on the opposite bank but stayed close.

After about an hour, we were still fishless. Bob caught up to me and said, "Hey, I have some things I have to do this afternoon. I was thinking we could hop out just upstream and then head out." He looked at me kind of intently, part confirmation, part question. I was pretty sure he didn't have anything else to get back to. It let me know how intentional he had been about this whole trip, to give me a little break from cancering, without forgetting how treatments were wearing me down. It was thoughtful, but I didn't want to go yet.

"Think I have time to fish this riffle by that log over there on the way out?"

"Just that one, and then I need to go." I nodded instead of rolling my eyes at him. *I'm fine!*

I fought my way upstream toward the log. Being entranced with executing my intentions with rod and line was hypnotic enough to satisfy in some ways, but I still wanted a fish. Three casts in, I felt the tug of a solid bite. I lifted my rod and held it high as the fish darted around sharply under the water in front of me. "Hey!" I called out to Bob. It was a meaty, healthy look- ing brown trout, a beautiful fish. I held it at the surface of the water and eased the hook from the side of its mouth. I admired it for a second, thanked it, and then let it go. I looked over to Bob and the other side of the river and smiled.

On the drive home, I leaned back into the headrest as Bob put context around our day's fishing into the patterns of the season, such a soothing way to think about time. I didn't realize how tired I was when we were in the river, but I felt every bit of it now and appreciated Bob cutting the day short.

I was waiting for Bob to ask about my decision to leave or stay at the Watershed Association. I figured it was coming, this talk. My indecision was putting a strain on the board, on the whole organization, and he was the middleman. We hadn't talked about it much recently, because, well, cancer. It con- founded my thoughts about everything. Coming to an honest decision would require separating pre-cancer perspectives on work from post-cancer ones. I'd get so far in the processing of it all and then my mind would simply shut off.

We were halfway home when I stopped waiting for the con- versation to shift. I relaxed further into the seat and just listened to Bob talk about fishing, about music, about nothing at all. This trip wasn't about getting to the bottom of my decision. Instead, Bob took a shot at anticipating what would make me feel better. The movement of water mimicked the passing of time, slow but not limited, in a way that carried me that day, in a way I didn't know I needed. Bob made it so that I didn't have to do anything difficult, just for a few hours. Instead, we spent time in a place that brought me peace. I learned in that moment a little bit more about what it means to be a good friend.

Look Past

Posted by Michele, April 17, 2012

Hey all,

I just heard from the radiation folks today and I start my six-week stint tomorrow. First appointment is 45 minutes. I think the rest of them will be around 20 minutes. To say that the radiation drive time alone is cramping my style is an understatement. But hey, think of all the things you can do on a road trip…. name that roadkill… practicing (loudly and with passion) for the next American Idol series… I'm going to Grandma's house and I'm bringing…. etc etc…

I posted weekly during radiation. Even when I asked people not to barrage me with questions, if I went too long without an update, they couldn't contain themselves, and I'd be cancering at meetings, in the grocery store, on the street. I'd rather control the narrative. I was well versed in the recipe.

At times it did feel like a chore. Because cancering is a chore. Not one that I signed up for and I never wanted to start a blog anyway. The reality was that updating everyone via my blog site consolidated the number of times I had to say those painful words. Those posts also gave me time for reflection. Time to work though how I wanted to navigate this on my own and as part of a wonderful community that rallies around each other. There was no rule that said I had to keep people updated. I did it because it was a way to let people in, yet still be in control of how far in. Still be in control of when to talk cancer. It spared us all the horribly uncomfortable moments when we've gone further than welcomed into another person's pain, that stumbling usually followed by a staggering retreat that makes everyone feel more alone.

By setting the bounds around a deeply personal, but safe zone, I could welcome the people around me. Posting those messages made me feel connected to everyone. Like we were all bearing witness to this thing together, counting down a defined number of steps to the finish line. It was a finish line we all wanted, we strove for it, and we got ready to celebrate my good fortune at the end. My posts had all been upbeat celebrations, a triumph or something to cheer. That I was making it, besting this thing with all my charms and wit, treatments and good luck. It was a trick to post the Goldilocks update that let people know how I was doing at the right level: not too personal, not too aloof, but just right.

Radiation is essentially throwing beams of intense energy at targeted areas with cancer. As my body would work to rebuild the cells destroyed during my six-week regime, the fatigue of radiation would be cumulative. I drove myself the 90-minutes each way for the first couple of weeks. Then we planned for Jon's family to come out for a week at a time to be my personal radiology chauffeurs. For all the years Jon and I have been together, we've been a plane ride away from our families. With both of our parents divorced, we have four separate households to visit. (That's four separate plane rides.) We spend nearly all our vacation time carving out space to try to visit each of them at least once a year.

Those visits have such weight when you're traveling so far for a short stay. Trying to get in all the fun. Trying to build and maintain connections sustained by phone calls until the next visit. Our families have connected over time, but you can only get to know each other so much in those small bits. With three hours of driving each day, we'd have more dedicated talk time than we ever had before.

Jon's sister, Coral, came out first. She'd drop me off at the radiology center building and circle the building for twenty minutes before picking me up for the ride home. One afternoon after treatment, we went down to the tennis courts near our house to casually bat the ball around. We'd just started playing, when Coral held up the tennis ball and said, "You know what, Michele? Let's pretend this ball is cancer."

Coral is a much better tennis player than I am. She could have smashed the crap out of that ball. But instead, she lobbed it gently over the net right to me. Swinging at that ball with everything I had made me forget I was tired for a moment, all that attention on something real and visible. Every once and a while, she'd stop and shake that tennis ball, looking like she might cry or scream, or both, an unspoken rant of everything that sucked about this mess. I saw her huge emotion and her struggle to contain it. I saw her disbelief at muddling through a tennis game with life-threatening illness hanging in the balance. I thought *Exactly, all of that, that's exactly it.* Feeling that connection instantly tied us together.

Another day, Coral and I shopped in a world market store where I found the most beautiful sarong in bright Mediterranean blue and lime green. We felt the delicious softness of its silk, and I pictured it transformed into the lightest curtains, blowing freely in my bedroom windows. I bought it because I needed the beauty, and because I wanted something to remind me of the week with her.

Jon's parents each took a week as well. By the time his mom, Linda, came out, I was well worn from radiation. Linda jumped right in, working so hard to bring love and relief to us all. She cleaned everything and tried to convince us that she liked doing it. One horribly gray and stormy day, we stood by the front door watching the rain blow sideways, and she said, "Isn't it beautiful?" I saw no beauty in the wet mess outside. "I love the rain," she continued. I tried to see it differently. But I didn't. Instead I looked around at a clean house, well-fed kids and all of her intention. "It is beautiful," I agreed.

Jon's dad, Leon, came out for the last week. One of the best parts of Leon being here was having him here for Jon. There is something about being around two people who truly adore each other. It brought me peace just to see Jon get filled up a bit, to see that joy without effort. Leon is an exceptional conversationalist, an extension of being a truly genuine man. He's sincerely interested in understanding your views, and why you think that way, and what that means. He asks all about you, without any judgement at all, in a way that makes you feel important and interesting. On our daily road trips, we talked a little bit about cancer, but more about other things. We talked about our lives now and how we got here. Jon's dad was a preacher, so I asked him about the differences among the denominations of Christianity. We looked up the difference between the British Isles, Great Britain, England and the United Kingdom. Having covered the big stuff, we were able to shift to lighter topics, to talk about things that were easy. Those weeks brought us, all of us, closer.

They got me through the thick of the treatments. I was completely off work at that point. I'd checked in with Bob regularly but still hadn't made a decision about whether or not I was coming back and in what role. I kind of knew at that point that I needed to step down, but there was a lingering thread that kept me from fully admitting it to myself. I loved the organization too much to do it the disservice of poor succession, so I'd toyed with planning the transition: the financial forecasting to set a salary and how long we could sustain it, the organizational shifts to dissect a job description carved specifically around me and mold it into something more hirable. But even the work of getting out of work made me tired.

Bob was trying his best to fill the void I left as director, and I could see how uncomfortable that was for him. But radiation was even more consuming than chemo, because I was literally surrounded by cancer treatment every day. I couldn't overcome the physical and emotional drain of it, so I left my decision hanging there, even more grateful that Bob didn't push for a decision from me.

For the last week of radiation treatment, I drove myself. The waiting room in the radiology center was grand and elegant. A full wall of windows from floor to ceiling lined the entire front of the building and looked out on to Lake Superior. I watched one freighter wait for its turn to enter the harbor and another further out in the lake. Those 1,000-foot ships were perched so delicately on top of an unusually calm Lake Superior it was like they were settled into a sheet of glass. The whole scene was so still, and with an endless horizon like possibility, that I wondered if time was passing at all. The contrast of color on either side of the clinic window was notable: all white and crisp in the waiting room, with the brilliant steely blue of the lake on the other.

There was a young woman, high school-aged, whom I had seen every day in the radiation center for the last few weeks. She never stopped to watch the lake. She didn't have a gown on like I did. She'd walk back into the radiation chamber with her regular street clothes on. A sheet of long hair that I was pretty sure was a wig wafted behind her. She always seemed to be in a desperate rush. She practically ran out of the radiation room. A football player-sized guy in a varsity jacket would hustle to catch up with her on the way out, his hands awkwardly shoved in his pockets. They never made eye contact with anyone, because they weren't really supposed to be here. They were supposed to be in gym class, or ecology club, or driving around finding new truths in bad pop music. Each day, she fled her radiation treatment as I was waiting for my own. The way she ran out of there broke my heart every time.

I thought about her having her first appointment with the radiation oncologist. I don't know what she was getting treated for. Her list of side effects was likely different, but I wondered if her doctor had laid out that list in the same way mine had. The doctor pulled up the seat next to me and settled in to explain this uncanny treatment: one you can't see or feel, but just magically happens through the air. He pulled out a blank piece of paper to carefully and thoroughly explained all the potential complications to worry about.

We were going to shoot beams of destruction at my body, so we'd need to set up the radiation to minimize damage to my heart and lungs. My breast would be forever hardened with thicker skin. I'd be more vulnerable to sunburn on that side. My skin would take a beating during treatment; we'd try to keep it intact, but it might open up, the skin dissolving. He described all these horrible things in a steady stream until he got to number seven, when I put my hand on the paper to stop him and said, "Please tell me you're not going to put an eight down on there."

He put his hand gently on my arm and said, "I am. And I'm going to write down a nine. And a ten."

I nodded slowly, felt myself deflate and said, "Okay."

I thought about how hard it had been to hear all of that at 37. I couldn't image hearing it at 17 or 18. Maybe the girl started running then and had never stopped. I watched the freighters on the lake for a while and then picked up a trashy entertainment magazine for distraction, hardly even looking at it. Someone began barking on the phone behind me. I flipped through my magazine and tried to ignore him, but he was in the seat directly behind mine and speaking loudly. There was no ignoring this guy. I managed to drown out the content, but I recognized the tone. He was sharp, efficient, and clearly in charge. There were only brief pauses before he'd jump back into giving orders with authority. He definitely expected action.

I think he got louder on the next call. There was some big work shakedown he was sorting out. His voice dominated the space. I grabbed another magazine and wondered if I'd hear him in the waiting room for the entire last week of my treatment.

Maybe he was taking time off work to drive someone here like Jon's family had done. It was distracting, and I found myself hoping that our timing wouldn't overlap.

I heard my name and stood up to follow the tech back to the radiation room. When I turned to gather my stuff, I saw the loud talker. Actually, I just saw the mass first. It was huge, bigger than a grapefruit and lodged on the side of his neck. I recoiled from it, from him, and was glad that he was facing the other way. The mass was shocking. I was unprepared for it because he didn't *sound* like someone with a grotesque and bulbous tumor. I looked away quickly and hurried after the tech.

I immediately recognized how drastically different I felt towards him before and after I saw his tumor. I thought about him going through his day with people either avoiding him entirely or unable to stop themselves from gawking. He must see those reactions; he must feel them every time in the same way I feel it when people look at me with pity, or fear, or discomfort. In the response of others, he's reminded of this horrible reality that he can't escape. With a tumor that big and visible, people couldn't help but see the illness first. But it's the same person on the inside there. When I was listening to him, I heard someone who was motivated and accomplished. Someone in charge and strong, and a little annoying. And the next second, I didn't see him at all. I saw a tumor, and it scared me so much I stopped looking for anything else.

I was struck by my opposing reactions to the man with the tumor and the young woman with the wig. All of us in that waiting room, seated or running, were there because we had cancer; his just happened to be on the outside. I'd had to stop myself from going to her, and I wasn't able to stop myself from running from him. And yet, I just finished a three-week stint where family came and doted on all things Michele. They saw me, not cancer, and I lolled around in their attention letting them fill me up. I was ashamed.

It was the last time I failed to look someone in the eye in a waiting room. Maybe they don't want any of my attention. That's okay, I'll leave them alone. But I will see them for themselves and not their disease. I'll look past the oxygen tanks, and the baldness, the hole in her throat, and the wheezing. I'll look past the fear and the age and say, "How's it going today?"

Done!

I was done. Chemo and radiation behind me, I could start carving out a way to move forward, to put closure on the treatment phase and move into the living-beyond-it phase. I sat to write a final post on my blog, a farewell to cancering updates. I had been keeping the posts upbeat and a few steps shy of tender intimacies, but close enough that they were real. Now that I was to write what I thought would be my last post, that balance felt even more delicate. So I leaned further inwards, allowed a slightly wider crack.

Posted by Michele, June 1, 2012

> *Well folks, I think this is by far my favorite message to write... now that the intensive treatment things are over with, I can focus on things that are in my control. Things that will help me to be healthy for longer. Makes me think about what it means to "Fight like a girl," which is actually*

a lot more subtle than I thought of before... it means that I will find a way to move cancer from this dominant place that it has been in my life for the last seven months, and I will assign it instead a little place of necessary attention, but no more. I will not let it scare me. I don't know how to do that yet. And so it goes... But maybe most importantly, fighting like a girl means I'm going to freaking enjoy myself! Ha! Take that stupid cancer.

A week after I finished radiation, I headed back to the cancer center in Ashland for a wrap up appointment with Mihailo. I asked, "Okay, so what kind of body scan do we do now? To see if all these treatments worked?"

"We don't."

I stared at him. We hadn't talked about post-treatment scans. I just assumed I would have one. It occurred to me just then that I'd never had a full body scan. We looked in my breast, and in the lymph nodes of my armpit, but not elsewhere. Maybe I was riddled with cancer. Maybe it was poking holes in my organs all over the place. How would I have the satisfaction of seeing a full body image that concludes *all clear*?

That we would walk away from this with no idea of the effectiveness of the chemotherapy and radiation made no sense to me. "Well, how do we know if it worked? I mean, don't we want to get some info here to see if we got it all?"

"Right," Mihailo nodded. "We've found that conducting scans doesn't have any influence on outcomes." The word "outcomes" refers to living or dying in cancering speak. A "good outcome" means surviving. A "poor outcome," well... they don't have to say "died." I winced at the word "outcomes." It failed to soften. Mihailo continued, "For the additional cost and exposure to radiation, scans haven't been shown to provide any benefits."

I scowled at him, confused. "Sooo, that's it? We just, do, nothing?"

"Well, not nothing." Mihailo described my post-treatment treatments in his steady, calm way. I'd have a mammogram every year. I'd be on hormone therapy to starve any remaining estrogen-feeding-cancer for the next five years - one small pill a day, minor side effects, hardly noticeable, just in case. An X-ray every six months would look for cancer in my lungs and ribs. "Breast cancer likes the bones," as Mihailo put it. Regular blood tests would look for signs that cancer was in my liver. He said these things like he wasn't afraid of them. But he spoke so gently, it was clear that he didn't forget that we were talking about my lungs, and my liver.

I listened intently, leaning forward to absorb every word. Grimacing, trying to fathom how I would walk out of that building without knowing. When he finished, we sat watching each other in a stalemate. He was waiting for me to process this, and I was trying to accept it. After a few minutes he said, "I realize this is one of the more dissatisfying things my patients hear."

I couldn't help but throw my head back and laugh, "Yeah, ya think so?!"

Mihailo grinned. "I'm open to talking about scans too, Michele. It's best to give it a little time after treatments. But we can order up a scan later."

For now, we would just coast. "Okay. So we just hope for the best here, huh?" I asked him.

"Yes," Mihailo said with all sincerity. "Yes, we do."

And then, on that lovely June day, I walked out of the clinic a cancer survivor. I was post-treatment, joining the ranks of the 250,000 women per year who walk out of some cancer center in the U.S. after some similar suite of treatment assaults. We're left to wonder if our futures will be cancer-free, starting with the day we finish treatments.

Summer

S ummer is the best time in the city, no doubt about it. She sits on the back rest of a park bench, her feet in flip flops resting on the seat of the bench. She leans back and crosses her legs to take in the view of the beach. There is nothing comfortable about the thin line of wood she sits on, but it doesn't matter. She loves it here. People are scattered all over the beach, in chairs or blankets in the sand. Beyond them, the ocean is subdued, the waves a gently rocking ebb and flow. Her whole crew is here. Surrounded by them, everything feels right in the world.

She sees him then about a block away; he's on his skateboard weaving his way through the narrow cracks in between people strolling the sidewalk. She watches them all jump as he passes and can't help but smile. Sure, it's obnoxious to ride through traffic that way, but his eyes are huge with focus and intensity. He is thriving on the challenge and win of never even touching the fabric of their clothes as he swerves by them. A rolling flash of agility and edginess. She silently cheers him on. *Good for you.*

When he gets closer to her bench, the sidewalk clears of targets to weave around. He stands and looks right into her; he knew she was here the whole time. She meets his gaze and raises her chin in a singular nod of acknowledgement. He returns it with a grin as he slows to a stop and picks up his skateboard. He can't hide the quick glance to the tallest skyscraper in the city, and in it, she sees the slightest crack in him as he sits down on the bench. She leans over to punch him playfully in the arm. *Come on friend. We don't have to Tango for months.*

She looks up across the ocean then and sees a sliver of the moon in the evening sky. It is contained, and they are here to enjoy the beach, and their friends, and themselves. They are here to see if they can find lightness, to see if they can recover and learn to trust again.

Uncertainty

I thought that the physical parts of cancer treatment would be the hardest. I thought that once I finished treatments, I would feel like I was done, and life would go back to the way it was. It didn't. The long list of unpleasant side effects was made small by the mental and emotional roller coaster of knowing that parts of me were changed forever, with no idea how healing would reveal bits of an unfiltered me. One unencumbered by the disease. Cancer survivors wear that title as a badge, rather a stain that can't wash off, an unwanted identity. It seemed like every moment held unwanted questions about how to wear that new identity. It was like I had been on sabbatical in a different cosmos that treasured reverence for living so highly that it took no time for granted. In that world, a love for the beauties of now were made greater and more fragile, because an un-promised future was a central tenant in the practice of living. Now I had to return to a world oblivious to how precarious our lives are, to a world filled with people who innocently assumed a security I could not feel. In contrast to my pre-cancer life, I felt completely new and raw, stymied by how I could re-enter with my outsides largely intact. But on the inside, I was roiling in evanescent uncertainties that churned so constantly I couldn't even feel them long enough to call them by name.

I started carving out a new normal, a return to life closer to what it was before, but not the same. After years of torturous waffling between staying as Executive Director and moving on, I resigned from my position without question. It wasn't a new perspective on the relevance of the career that I'd been tirelessly advancing for decades. I left because I knew the constant push of time and energy that the position demanded, that the organization deserved. There are no non-profits that stay afloat with directors lacking commitment. Fully invested directors put in 60-hour weeks as a base and more when needed without hesitation. I didn't know how to be a director any other way. But now, giving that much of my time to a job was as absurd as giving away my daughters. I felt that truth without question, through every pore. My time became far more valuable. Work got smaller.

And then, there was the need for health insurance. We didn't provide health insurance through our organization, and neither did Jon's job as a real estate agent. Since we were still poor enough, we qualified for a state-run option, but we continually wavered on the cusp of qualifying income. Make another hundred dollars this month, and we'd get bumped off. With a pre-existing condition (pre-Affordable Care Act), we'd really be screwed.

That used to be a smaller stress. A "worth it" stress overshadowed by the change I could create in my work. Before cancer, health insurance was nominal, an unnecessary safety net we'd never use since we were completely healthy and assumed we always would be. After cancer, work became a means to a beginning. I helped the board with financial and organizational planning to hire a new leader. I worked with them to outline the most important hard skills and natural talents to look for in a successful director. I even sat in on the first round of interviews. Then I moved on. I found a fisheries job locally working on Lake Superior and her feeder streams. A job I still felt deeply inspired by, yet not consumed by like I had been. And it provided health insurance.

At three months post-treatment, my hair started growing back. I took my hormone therapy pill every morning, watching attentively for its side effects, but there weren't many. I looked for any signs of cancer returning, having no idea what cancer's return would feel like. Mihailo told me to pay attention to a new pain, or any new sensation, guidance so sufficiently vague it instilled a penetrating and constant focus on every sensation.

Even a series of toe stubbing held potential. I stubbed my toe three times in a month. *Three times!* It may seem, at first, clearly ridiculous to tie toe-stubbing to cancer. But hold on, it's less ridiculous than it could be. One of the potential side effects of my chemo was neuropathy, the loss of feeling in your fingers and toes. I thought I could feel my toes. I could feel them whenever I poked at them. But stubbing my toe that often was something *new*. At my next appointment, I gave Mihailo just enough time to say hello before I blurted out, "I stubbed my toe three times in the past month."

He sat down on his little rolly stool and said, "Oh no."

"Yeah, it really hurt." I said. He nodded in agreement of the ouch of toe-stubbing. "Twice on my right foot and once on the left," I continued, gesturing towards my feet thinking *There it is.*

There's the symptom. There's the something new. I waited for a long medical explanation and that would lead into a relevant enlightening of... something. We'd probably need a scan now.

Instead, he just pushed his glasses up and said, "That's too bad." I waited. Mihailo waited. Until I started to laugh with the realization it was non-cancer related toe stubbing. Just me being pretty darn clumsy.

So what does cancer pain feel like? Mihailo told me to take notice of an unexplained, persistent, non-symmetric pain. Bodies are weird though. We have irregular little discomforts of muscle strain, or indigestion all the time. He said to wait two weeks if such a pain surfaced. I watched him hard as he said this, thinking that two weeks seemed like an awfully long time to let cancer eat away at my innards. Because catching cancer early, should it return, was key. A new uncertainty to live with, I turned to Mihailo's guidance often in an attempt to find the impossible balance between *Constant vigilance!* and *Don't be obsessed!*

I turned to rebuilding the foundation of a non-cancery life. I went to brunch at a friend's house soon after I finished my first rodeo of treatments. I knew all the women there, but none of them well. They were a group that got together regularly for this brunch, rotating houses. I was invited as a new guest, and I looked forward to it, interested to get to know all of them more.

We settled in around the feast, and I watched as they lobbed anecdotes about non-cancery lives with kids across the table. I followed these sunny little stories from woman to woman, recognizing a lightness that I only then realized I didn't have. As I sat listening, every small story of a life yet untainted of an un-promised future made me feel my own heaviness more acutely.

One of the women was pregnant. She was in the later stages of pregnancy when you're so big that the presence of the baby pushes your organs into places they don't normally rest. *I was reading that at this stage my stomach is all the way over here. Isn't that amazing?* What did that remind me of that I could offer to the evolving conversation? *I was recently thinking about my organs too! I was thinking about being really still during radiation so that they didn't hit my heart if I breathed in too deeply.* I skipped that cheerful contribution and tried to find something non-cancery to contribute. There was nothing.

As the brunch wore on, I felt less and less able to be a part of it. I put on a plastic smile that felt as fake as it was to join their fun. Now 38, I was the first of my peers to have such a serious illness, and my energy didn't fit. It's not that I wasn't welcome; my life was just so *different*. They'd talk about how many more children they wanted to have, and I'd think about the hormonal medication that sent me in to early menopause. They'd talk about diaper rash, and I'd think about that horrible breakout that covered my scalp when the detached stubble of my hair poked a small infection in every pore. The anxiety of trying to fit into a life that would never again be mine continued to build until I burst into sobs at a topic as benign as a new kitchen remodel project. I tried to explain myself, pausing every half sentence to gasp for air. I didn't intend to derail the brunch from its happy chatter; it just jumped up on me, and I couldn't contain it. I was really losing it, like slobbery crying, and looked up to see five faces with wide eyes staring back at me, completely unprepared for this. I was still in my sabbatical in the cancery cosmos. They had no idea how to console me back to earth. And I had no idea how to be a part of it without letting my reality gush out and flood the room. I was never invited to another brunch again.

Isolation

Another year passed, and my appointments stretched from three to six-month intervals. We settled into our new home; the girls settled into their new school. My X-rays and mammograms all came back clear. I still kept wondering if the treatments had worked.

In that first year after finishing treatments, cancer was so fresh, stayed so close the surface, that any topic broke the skin. I didn't know how to keep it light, and I couldn't have conversations about the heavy. As a result, I felt like an imposter in any conversation. *Hey! I know we're hanging out talking about gardening, but I had cancer!* But that was the thing. My thoughts about gardening, about anything, were refracted by cancer. I loved to garden before I got cancer, and I loved it after. But how I loved it was drastically different. Before, I loved the work, the big end product I could sit back and admire. But after cancer, gardening became about being present, about the process, and the little parts of it. Gardening was about a cup of coffee on a

Saturday morning, and finding the little flower hiding under the dogwood. It was about seeing the subtle beauties in the details, and at the same time about just feeling that I was right there in the garden, nowhere else.

It took me years to talk about hostas without first painting this backdrop of cancer and how it's changed my view of it. Because mostly people just want to talk about hostas.

I felt the distance as an untenable connection when talking about happy things, but also when talking about other people's hard times as well. I became the standard of shittiness, the epitome of "It could be worse…" I could even see the moment when people felt their foot in their mouth. They'd start backpedaling about how a broken water heater isn't really that big of a deal.

Some days, when I wasn't feeling very open, I'd let them squirm in a silence that said, *Yeah, and you're complaining to a living example of how much worse things can be.*

Those were days when I didn't have the energy to be generous, or compassionate. I hated that this was true. On my low days, I felt righteous in deserving more than half the empathy in every conversation. But that was a hollow way to live, only listening through a filter that evaluates the worthiness of someone else's experience based on my own. It was in those moments that I felt like cancer was winning, when I started turning into someone I'm not.

But talking to those who could relate didn't work either. There was a man who worked at the pharmacy where I filled my prescriptions. After a while, he didn't have to ask for my name. I didn't know if that was endearing or sad. When the man recognized my medication as the same one his wife took 20 years ago, he would tell me stories about her. I didn't welcome it, but I needed the prescription, so I listened. He told me she stopped wearing head scarves before her hair fully grew back. *The guts that took*. He'd smile and shake his head like it was the first time he'd ever mentioned it. And every month I'd play along like it was the first time I've ever heard it, because it was his way of trying to make me feel like I was going to be okay.

I saw him at the post office the other day. He said that his wife had died recently. Her cancer came back aggressively, and it didn't take long until it overcame her. He was adjusting. He was at the post office sending gifts to his grandkids, a role he had taken over now that she was gone. He was walking around with an open wound of grief and an armful of packages to be sent. It was such a raw intimacy, right there in the line at the post office.

Cancer tugged at both ends, making it tough to find comfort with the happy, well-adjusted people, or with the sad people either. I didn't fit anywhere. In a small town, I would run into people I knew at every turn and would try to keep the conversation to three sentences until I'd stammer out an excuse to move on. I found myself pulling away from my community for fear of having a real conversation with anyone.

But the more I sheltered myself from other people's stories, the more alone I felt. Without an open and real connection, I was only getting filtered conversations based on "what's appropriate to talk about to the woman with cancer." More importantly, I realized what a small fraction of humanity I was experiencing. I was missing out on what people were thinking and feeling, the real stuff that comes from deep in the core, from the heart. It left me with shallow, empty talks, when what I needed was the opposite. I had to re-train myself to listen for the purpose of understanding and appreciating other people, recognizing that their stresses and challenges are different yet equally valid as my own. I didn't have a corner on the market of hard times. I learned that I had to be the one to invite that relationship to get reacquainted after cancer, so they knew it was okay to tell their own story without reserve. I had to open that door or be left stranded behind cancer's shroud.

I found the ones who wanted the backdrop. The ones who could bear all the gritty details because they knew I needed to release them. The ones that could come to a place where words like 'cancer' were to be spoken freely, the depth of those relationships made more intensely beautiful by willingness. It wasn't until after I was past the tornado of treatments that I could fully see the willing, the ones who helped pick up all the vulnerabilities I laid down. The ones who showed up—who first showed up—and weren't scared off when I put words to this thing. How much I needed them, people to receive the words of my reality. Because when I said something out loud, it gave it shape and weight enough that we could look at it from different angles. They made it so I didn't have to weed through this unwanted experience alone. It was so grounding, so wonderfully comforting, to be tethered securely enough that I wouldn't float off into Neverland trying to find this new me, yet given enough rope when it was hard to see.

In the years that followed my treatments, the grounding I felt most came from my sister. We never did go through rounds of reconciliation talk. Instead, against every fiber of her being, she squelched her need to talk it all through to make room for mine. With that, I was able to open up more and then able to see her more clearly.

Before, I was overcome with the wild parts of Heather, preoccupied with comparing myself to her, and how I didn't measure up. I wasn't as funny, as engaging. The way she commanded attention made me feel irrelevant. I *never* felt irrelevant in my other relationships. I didn't consciously blame my insecurities on her. Instead, I stopped trying to get a word in, and assumed the position of wall flower as she led the show.

But she showed up for cancer. And kept showing up. I went out to Colorado to visit a few summers after my first treatments were finished. We stopped in her classroom, the same room she's been teaching middle school English in for the last 20 years. It's a position that she says fits her well because she's at the same maturity level of her students. *Oh, I can out-crazy your teenager, easily.* The walls were littered with her student's work and posters with quotes like, "Everything you do throughout the year is a brushstroke, and how you fill in your canvas is completely up to you."

"Oh! And here's the best part!" she told me, plugging her iPod into the wall. Angsty teenager music came pounding through speakers, and she started throwing down some jagged dance moves. "I *love* Twenty-One Pilots." She kept grooving and shouted over the jam, "I play this when my students come in to get them in the mood!" I stood there awkwardly, but soon started swaying around too, right there in an 8th grade classroom. Heather has that effect on people, with and without trying.

She turned down the music to tell me about her students. The ones that have model behavior but put out no effort. The ones that come to her when there is abuse at home. The ones that are lost in being 13 years old and can't find their voice. She speaks differently when she talks about them. She is softer and more genuine. I saw then that there is intention in what seems light and carefree. While she's on stage with big energy thriving at the center her students' attention, she's also watching every single kid, to see who they really are without throwing a spotlight on them. Her atypical, adult theatrics served to loosen them up, so she could focus on knowing each of them fully. Well, unless she's really got a class laughing, then she might just be working the room.

I saw, for the first time, how both those things - the extrovert feeding repartee and the immense compassion for people's most intimate needs - can be present at the same time. I realized that she has been paying attention all along, more so than I had been. I was not proud of that.

As we were driving back to her place from the school, she told me about a friend of hers who fell on hard times. Her friend kept retreating from her problems, spending more time in bed and less taking care of her own kids. At first, a crew of friends reached out to help, bringing meals and stopping by. Months later, most stopped going over as they shifted from empathy to judgement. But Heather kept bringing meals; she drove her friend's sons to their practices. She bought them shoes when she saw a toe poking through the tip. She questioned how much was enough, where the line was between support, enabling, and being taken advantage of, but she kept going over because she saw a family in need. She supports the people she loves when it's easy, but also when it's not.

I only came to know these things after cancer, after the reconciliation. It horrifies me to think that maybe I never would have known her, my sister. I saw that love is all the details big and small. It's what we find when we take the time enough to slow down and pay attention. And I realized that I hadn't been paying attention. I still don't know what's beyond the stage of my sister's big presence and humor. I don't know what makes her tick.

I started paying attention to the details, the intricacies that make each of us uniquely ourselves. Because love is in the specifics. I didn't want to miss any of them.

Wendy, What to Say?

It was almost five years after my first diagnosis; a significant milestone because if you make it to five, you're more likely to make it to ten. At ten years, your chances of getting cancer are the same as those who have never had it before. This is considered "cured" in cancer world. I was starting to feel more confident, cancer further in the rear view; I didn't see it as much on the road ahead of me. Some days I even forgot that it had ever been a passenger, but the car still held the leftover smell of it, a faint stench I knew I'd never be fully rid of.

On a Saturday afternoon, I sat in our school's gym watching my girls play in a volleyball tournament. They were in sixth grade then and had been drawn to volleyball immediately. Their desire was beyond their ability, but they were driven to contribute to our small school's reputation as a top contender in our conference each year. They practiced as much as they could: at school recess, in the backyard, at organized practices. Today was their first tournament, the energy of it fresh and new to both them and to me.

The gym was wide enough to host two games simultaneously, filling the gym with the chaotic symphony of volleyball. Parents in the stands cheered for their daughters. Sneakers squeaked on the shiny wood floor. There was a constant rhythmic boom of volleyballs getting passed, a short-lived tempo that ended with the different tone of a volleyball hitting the floor and referees whistling short blasts. At regular intervals, the shrill chorus of young, hormone-filled girls outdid it all as they screamed victory for a point made. The music of volleyball is a dissonant jamboree of big emotion.

I sat waiting for the girls' turn to play. I saw their coach, Wendy, lead our team like little ducklings to the court, a floor that is named after her as the "Meierotto Court" in honor of the 25 years she and her husband coached here. The gym walls were lined with banners of championship victories, the teams of which included either her sister or daughters. Amidst the riotous racket of overlapping volleyball games, Wendy appeared utterly calm, unfazed by the jumble of sound and action.

When we started to play, Wendy stood on the sidelines offering some correction after nearly every point. The girls looked to her constantly, desperate to get it right, to earn her approval. During one play, the other team hit the ball on a high, arching path over the net. It skyrocketed right towards the edge of the court. Wendy saw that our team was paralyzed with indecision— was the ball out of bounds? or in?—and immediately her rich booming voice filled the gym, a growling roar over all the other background noise: "PLLLLAAAAAAY IIIT!" The entire gym screeched to a halt, and that play became the center of it all. Our players froze, paralyzed as the ball hit the ground, in bounds.

They looked sheepishly at Wendy, apologetic and a whole lot intimidated. Until Wendy started to laugh, "Alright, girls, this one. Let's get this one." Wendy was tough. She was in command. She had the respect of everyone in the gym.

Wendy fully understood the role model she was for her players and did not underestimate the responsibility of it. She embodied what she worked to instill: hard work, integrity, respect for self and others, and kindness. She often ended practice by tasking the team to do something nice for someone else in the upcoming week. When the next practice came around, she'd gather them up and ask for reports on their acts of kindness: a compliment given, sitting with someone at the lunch table that had been on their own, donating to the local food shelf. Volleyball was about winning, absolutely. But for Wendy, it was also about inspiring young women to be the best of themselves. She did this practice after practice, season after season, for decades.

My girls adored Wendy. She's one of the few people I've met strong enough to stand toe-to-toe with Caitlin. Caitlin is remarkably and beautifully stubborn. Channeled in the right way, this will be one of her best traits. I can't wait to see what she does with it. However, as a young teen, that morality often leans libertarian. On more than one occasion she's nearly talked me out of doing her chores with shrewd, convincing arguments delivered with absolute certainty. Finding the right thing to fight for is a learned trait. We didn't quite have it down yet.

After practice one day, Wendy marched towards me; She was fired up. As soon as she reached me, she fumed that every time she'd offer any sort of coaching, Caitlin would reject it, explaining how her way was better.

"She doesn't tell *me*," Wendy said with command, "how to play volleyball."

I worked not to smile, but I think one snuck out anyway. "I know," I said nodding. "We're working on that." In a second, there was an immediate shift. I saw Wendy recognize that she had an opportunity to help a young woman learn that respect doesn't mean conceding your own importance. Wendy had the same fearless qualities as Caitlin herself; they may have been equally as stubborn. Wendy was what Caitlin needed.

Wendy's effect on Lily was just as strong. After Lil had a tough game, I watched Wendy drape her arm around Lil's shoulders, talking softly to her as they walked slowly around the court. Lily soaked in every drop and swelled with confidence from receiving Wendy's full attention. She came downstairs the next morning full of the warmth of it.

"G'morning Bug. Want some coffee?" I asked as Lil rubbed her eyes.

Still groggy with a steaming mug at the table, she said, "I had the greatest dream last night," looking wistfully off into the distance, "that Wendy was my mom."

"Oh." I said, forcing myself not to react as I flipped the eggs I was making her for breakfast. "That sounds like a really great dream, Lil."

"It was," she agreed. "You know when you wake up from a dream that was so good you wish it was real?" She said this with the assumption that I'd *totally* be able to relate. She was wishing herself back there as she took another sip of the coffee *I* had made for her.

I tried to see the good in having another strong female role model for my daughter and tried not to take it personally. Instead, I blurted out, "Wendy doesn't let her kids drink coffee."

"What?" Lily was pulled from her wistful daydream. I could feel her looking at me with a scowl but said nothing, kept stirring the eggs. "How do you know that?"

"She probably pinches her kids when they're sleeping too."

"Whatever, Mom," she said as she walked out of the room.

I was on my way into the gym for the next volleyball game when another parent told me that Wendy had been diagnosed with cancer. Wendy's persistent cough over the past few months wasn't a stubborn cold; it was lung cancer. I was instantly transported back to the fear and shock of my own new diagnosis. Imagining the weight of it for Wendy and her family thickened the air. It made me want to run out of the gym so I wouldn't have to see Wendy. I wouldn't know what to say. You'd think I would.

I forced myself to stay and found a seat with the other parents on our team's side of the bleachers. We were half watching the game and half watching Wendy sit quietly in her coach's chair with her arms crossed in front of her. The steady stream of whispers - *Did you hear? Do you know anything else?* - opened the sore spot of being the subject of sharp attention, knowing that the hum of whispers was about you. I felt like a pressure cooker pushed to the edge of what it could contain. I wanted to erase it all violently. I sat apart from the other parents hating the moment, forcing myself not to flee, and trying to think of what to say to Wendy.

I knew with certainty the things not to say. It's easier to list these things off. Don't talk about all the people you know who have died from cancer, clearly. Don't pry for personal information to satisfy your own curiosity. *How big is the tumor?* Umm, no, don't ask that. Consider your timing. Making some small, fleeting comment after the game might make me feel like I've done *something*, but it's not really helpful. I sat replaying all the things from my own experience that I wanted to avoid. No comments of pity, no defeat.

The reality was that I knew I couldn't talk to her without crying. I couldn't even get near her without crumbling in sadness and empathy and anger and fear. I'd be a sobbing mess, putting Wendy in the position of having to console me. I couldn't do that. So instead, I avoided her.

It was horrible to avoid her. But I did. For weeks. I didn't know how to be supportive on the giving side of cancer, instead of the receiving side.

My first thought was of Heather, and her wonderful ability to bring light without minimizing, both halves of that equation were essential and made me feel safe. She always saw me, not cancer. Heather waited until I felt like talking, and never presumed how I should feel or think. And she always followed my lead. If I felt like sobbing, she cried with me. If I was angry, she was angry with me. If cancer didn't come up, she didn't go there. But she wouldn't follow me down a *I'm now going to sit on the couch and mope for the rest of my life* kind of lead. Instead, she'd acknowledge every feeling and then provide the bumpers. For years I'd been trudging along on the receiving end of her giving as status quo and only then realized what a fine line it was to walk.

My sister.

Wendy does have sisters, and I'm not one of them. I'm not in her inner circle. I had experienced casual acquaintances that assumed they were welcome to pry into my most painful intimacies. It often wasn't received as intended. The intensity of cancer was too much. Their well-intentioned intrusion thickened my wall of privacy to protect myself.

I looked to my experiences with my outer circle of friends, a cancer relationship with a much different tenor. Initially, I couldn't receive the good intentions of the people around me. I left each conversation as soon as I could, feeling burdened to be the gracious cancer patient. I didn't have the strength to receive their support, didn't feel open enough, or simply wanted to talk about non-cancery things. Instead, I felt barraged by the constant reminder of *Cancer! Cancer! You have cancer!*

Still, I felt guilty for not holding up my end of the bargain, for avoiding people often. I mentioned this to a close friend, and she stopped me immediately, "Girl, you have cancer. You get it your way."

It was liberating, feeling that truth instantly. It's not the way I normally go through life. *Hi everyone. I'm here, and I get it my way.* But we're talking about cancer here. So of course I get it my way. Hard to figure what you want "your way" to be when you're thrown into the middle of a shitstorm, and you can't stop to think. I knew I didn't want to shut people out—inner or outer circle. But I needed boundaries. I sent a message out through my website to "get it my way."

Posted by Michele, December 6, 2011

I was just thinking about these updates… and how cancer's kind of awkward - what do you say to the cancer woman? S,o let's hop right over the awkward-conversation-with-a-lady-who-has-cancer thing like this. If I bump into any of you out and about and I feel like shit, I probably won't want to talk about it. And if I bump into you wherever and I feel like a normal person, then I probably won't want to talk about cancer either. So, let's just pretend that I didn't have cancer and chit chat like it's any other day. We can even smile at the funniness of that as we do. Because belittling cancer like it ain't no thing, makes me feel stronger than it. That would be helpful. I write this with gratitude for all of your support and caring and hope that it will help us muddle through this as best we can. I hope it's received like that.

My inbox was flooded with messages. Confessions like *I always feel like I'm saying the wrong thing,* or *I feel like you won't think I care if I don't ask.* The honesty brought us closer. Sharing vulnerabilities in a deeper place of connection and allowed for more of it. A woman who I knew through my work started sending me short emails. She found happy things to talk about, each one including something that made me feel like the person I was before cancer. She didn't ask for anything in these emails. Not for details. Not for a response. They were pure giving, and it allowed me to let down my guard and open up. I hardly knew her when we started swapping messages. To this day, I'm not sure I could pick her out in a crowd. But I feel like I know her—her sincere generosity—and love her for it.

But would any of these things help Wendy? There are too many dials on any given moment, on any given person, to prescribe a flow chart of the perfect thing to say to the friend with cancer. The things that made me feel better might do the opposite for her. We differ too much in our needs and personalities and moods of the moment. But we can show up in a way that is genuine. We can be there without assuming we know exactly what will be helpful. We can follow their lead. We can listen.

I started going out of my way to just say hi to Wendy. I made myself available. I'd try to be light and casual and talk about anything but cancer. There were times when she'd turn to greet me, and her subtle sigh and stiff posture made it clear she was bracing for unwanted cancer questions. I'd immediately lead the conversation elsewhere.

One Saturday morning, I walked into the gym to pick up the girls from volleyball and saw Wendy and her sister in the middle of the court. When they looked my way, I saw Wendy assume the bracing-for-cancer-talk position, so I got extra casual when I reached them, "Hey, how's it going?"

We talked weather. We talked volleyball. I asked how Caitlin was doing and Wendy said, "Better. I think we've come to an agreement about who's in charge here."

"I'm glad to hear that," I smiled. "Hey, Lily had a dream about you the other night." Wendy looked at me apprehensively. "It was kind of funny actually." I recounted Lil's dream, embellishing Lil's wistful gaze into the distance. Wendy alternated between laughing along and grimacing in empathy as a fellow mom.

When we finished a good laugh over the dream, Wendy raised her eyebrows and exhaled, "I thought you were going to say that she had a dream that I died."

We left the laughter behind. I waited, and then only managed, "That would not be a funny dream."

"No, it wouldn't." She shook her head once.

I tried to build her up. "All Lil sees is how much she adores you. I think any one of these girls could have had that dream."

Wendy nodded, looking at the floor. I didn't know if I should invite more, allow her to let the scary thoughts out. Was the middle of the gym with teens all around the place for that? Wendy's mantra for fighting cancer was *Winning is the Only Option*. She was fiercely unwavering in the belief of her survival. I tried to build on that and said, "This is such a great bunch of girls. I can't wait to see them get even better."

Wendy looked up and said, "They are. I just hope I'm around to be here with them." I felt the familiarity of these thoughts sneaking in. When you'd like to be in the moment, but cancer abruptly bounces up and down in your face, so you can't see past it. It is surreal to be in that space in between cancer's ugly and the brightly colored future promised to everyone else. The redirection, redirection, is isolating. Sometimes it's a relief to just say your fears instead of pretending like they're not there.

I hoped it was cathartic for her to let it out.

"Yeah, I hope so too."

Wendy made eye contact with me again and nodded with acknowledgement of her cancer diagnosis and mine, "We're both hoping for that."

"Yes. We are. I've been thinking so much about you, Wendy."

Moving on

A s I got further away from treatments, I spent less time in the cancer center. Which only made me want to spend even less time at the cancer center and more time among the cancer-free. Away from the cancery reminders of tests and needles and appointments. The full body test I considered years ago held less of an appeal. The data shows that additional testing doesn't affect outcomes, right? Probably not even necessary. But the persistent, low-grade anxiety of not knowing whispered, *Get a scan! Get it!*

I decided not to. The assurance I was looking for wouldn't be satiated with a scan. First, the scans aren't 100 percent accurate. My MRI going into my first surgery only picked up one lump, but there were another two. I could get a scan now and still wonder if I was really clear. Even if I did trust it, I'd start wondering in a few months if cancer had started growing since then. What I really wanted, was complete certainty that I was going to be okay. I wasn't going to get it. The uncertainty was always going to be there.

I've been asked, *How do you deal with not knowing*? Since there was no option to live without it, I just did. I leaned on the guidance from Mihailo to ignore a fleeting pain. I trusted my X-rays and blood tests. Mostly though, I leaned on the numbers. A 90-percent survival rate, leading to a cure was a pretty good number. When I'd get a little nervous about that other ten percent, I'd remind myself of the marvels of science and all the new treatments in development that would be available to treat the unlucky few. But it wouldn't be me anyway. I'd be fine. When that didn't work, I'd remind myself of what was real around me right now, in this very moment, the things I knew, instead of fixating on the things that scared me. Some days I limped along faking it. But as time went on, there were more days when I didn't even have to try. I never wanted to practice this, but simple repetition made it more bearable. More than anything, I *got used to* being a cancer survivor.

Fall

They stand together at the edge of the roof listening to the gentle rhythm of waves rolling across the beach beyond it. A reminder of the life they knew before Tango, before they ever stepped onto this rooftop. She can already feel the stress of another night's dance. She doubts if she has enough left to muddle through the dance. She looks up for a last glimpse of tonight's stars before they are erased by the light of the moon. As if it heard her, the moon begins its climb. Even a glance at its edges is untenable, worse yet when it is fully exposed, and perches itself comfortably atop the neighboring building. Like it or not, there is Tango to dance tonight.

On cue, music fills the rooftop, and they reluctantly assume their positions. She is limp, knowing that dancing well will serve her better, but she can't muster enough focus. Normally, he would provide more structure when she needs it, but he has nothing more to give. They go through the motions halfhearted. An elbow sags. The sweep of leg not quite as wide. A turn to shift direction a little bit late. The frame of their bodies not as rigid as the dance would like. A bit lazy, they trudge on with enough resolve to show up but lacking the passion of Tango.

The moon maintains its ever-present glow, commanding the night sky. Through all their dancing, they have been obsessed, repulsed, and infuriated by it. Alternately, and simultaneously. They've spent hours studying every crack and fissure, relentlessly searching for a revelation in every shade, every angle. But an unsolvable puzzle wears after time. The moon gives up no secrets. It is a defiant ball of enigmatic rock.

They start to Tango on the far side of the roof, to get as far away from the moon as possible. Unspoken intention simply leads them away. They catch the slightest glimpse of the beach as they pass the edge of the roof, and both of them feel the deep longing to be there, not here. They can hear the ocean's soft murmur under the whine of Tango's music. Tomorrow, they will walk the shore with the soft sand between their toes. They will swim in the waves with their friends and love it. They will feel the sun on their skin and love it. They will feel the ocean's salty breeze and love it. And they'll not be able to shake the moon.

The Second Rodeo

I t took a while to dawn on me, the second round of cancer. The warning signs were subtle and readily explained by something else. Cancer took it's time sneaking back without comment for a few months.

I tried to be an enlightened cancer patient the second rodeo, one who knows not to get ahead of herself. It's hard to know where the line is between preparing and obsessing. I told myself I was researching simply to become a well-informed patient. I denied that it was desperation to make a horror story less terrifying by unveiling all its jump scares, to assure myself that I'd end up okay.

I replayed the conversations with the mammogram nurse six months earlier. How I told her that the offending breast, especially the skin on this inside section, seemed more taut, That it was red, and hot. Seemed swollen. *Nothing to worry about*, she said, *radiated breast tissue is just like that sometimes*. She was wrong.

Maybe I could have taken all my self-actualized, dealing-with-cancer tricks and plow right through a nice friendly Stage II cancer again. I'd know the rules, the strategies. It would be well-defined. But the game had changed. There were some similarities, but this cancer wasn't the same at all; it was far more menacing.

Jon approached the second rodeo in the same way he handled the first. Jon is an enlightened cancer supporter. He didn't have to talk himself back from getting ahead. He just didn't jump there in the first place. Jon listened to whatever I'd been researching and the new insights that might or might not be relevant but didn't get emotionally invested. He stayed firmly rooted in, "Well, let's see what Mihailo has to say."

It was really the only thing to do, but his lack of shared panic was wholly unsatisfying. Jon does best when he responds to something known. When it comes to pouring over all possible treatments for all possible scenarios, he's not my go-to guy.

For that, I called my sister. I called her from my car after every appointment. I don't know how I went through the first round without her on the daily. I'd leave the shared office space of my coworkers and stand outside my building to unload every update: an appointment made, preliminary results and a follow-up scheduled, a first indication that didn't look so bad, another test scheduled. But then the results started to reveal the true nature of this cancer. Each new layer unfolded implications that left me engulfed in a desperate, panicked sadness.

What a gift it is to have someone who will just be sad with you. Someone who knows it is not the time to find an answer, or make it better, or solve your problem. But someone who will just be there with you when you are so very devastated. I appreciated her silence, interrupted only by sobbing that she tried to muffle.

The love in holding back her own pain to allow more space for mine did not lose itself on me.

When I got the results that my cancer had spread, I wept to Heather, "I would have made a fantastic grandmother." She cried with me harder. Because it's true. I would be a grandmother of epic proportions. The play, the tenderness, the attention would be so phenomenal, no grandchild ever, anywhere, would ever be so loved. How desperately I mourned the loss of a Gammy for my unborn grandchildren. Of not knowing what my daughters' faces would look like the first time they looked into her their child's eyes. I don't know what was harder. Thinking about missing my time in the lives of my family, or simply not knowing what their lives would entail.

When I couldn't bear to think about the future anymore, I switched to regret.

Maybe I could have caught it in time if I had been more adamant about how itchy the breast was. The scans came back clear though, so I disregarded my doubts. When that mild itch grew to a horrible discomfort with scabby skin, I called the cancer center. They recommended seeing a family practice doctor, who attributed it to a yeast infection, common to nursing mothers. I even applied the lotion a few times before my trust dissolved at this ridiculous diagnosis, and I went to the cancer center for the oncology nurses to take a look. I could see it in their faces immediately. It wasn't a yeast infection. It was typical radiated breast tissue. I had every sign. "I don't like it when you guys look worried," I said a little louder than I meant to. One of them hugged me hard and walked me directly to the nurse's station to schedule an appointment.

"His schedule is booked," said the receptionist.

"Make room." said my nurse. That's when I knew. This was happening, again.

The biopsy came back as inflammatory breast cancer. Meaning it wasn't a distinct tumor buried in a nice neat ball somewhere the inside. We couldn't just go take it out. It was in my skin like water, without defined edges. That itch, the heat, the pressure was from cancer actively spreading. The scabby scaring spreading across my breast was cancer, right there on the surface in broad daylight.

It was the interior places we were even more worried about. My breast didn't function to keep me alive. My liver did though. Mihailo walked into the exam room quickly with the CT scan results. Before he even made it to his chair he said, "I'm worried, Michele. I'm worried." We scrolled through the black and white images of the CT scans. They were in series like I was a loaf of bread and the pictures were slices of me from chest to hips. The nodes around my heart were inflamed, a few more in my armpit. All the spots in my liver were most concerning. "Too numerous to count," the report said. I found that a little insulting. So many tiny spots it wasn't even worth tallying them. How would I know when there were fewer spots? We'd need a biopsy of those dark spots in my liver to be sure.

"What will we do if the biopsy comes back negative?" I asked Mihailo.

His shoulders sagged with what he already knew. "We'll get another biopsy, from one of the other spots." Oh. So, we're kind of that sure.

The liver was hot. The day I got the official diagnosis, Jon and I sat on the couch in the living room that evening while I googled stage IV inflammatory breast cancer. The girls were in and out of the room, so I'd quickly scan my phone for a few minutes at a time. I couldn't wait for a more private time. I was dying (yes, that's cancer humor right there, folks) to know what I was dealing with. *Mom, where's the mac and cheese?* Inflammatory breast cancer is rare, accounting for only one to five percent of all breast cancers. *I can't find my volleyball shoes, Mom!* It's even more rare for a solid tumor to come back in an inflammatory form. *Why doesn't she have to do the dishes? I did them last time.* It's typically diagnosed in younger women, and it is very aggressive. The average life expectancy is eighteen months.

Eighteen months.

I gasped at the words *eighteen months.* I couldn't breathe at the words *eighteen months.* Jon saw me react and leaned in to see. I held up the phone and waited while he read. I saw exactly when he read *eighteen months.* He stopped breathing, then looked to me. We stared deep into each other with no tears, but wide, wet eyes. I saw his raw fear in an instant: the absence of me. For us, for him, for the kids. I have never loved him more than in that moment, yet I instantly felt like he was on the far end of a hallway that stretched longer and longer every second. I wanted to crawl on top of him and hold on with every bit of strength I had. I'd lace my fingers and my ankles around him, and I'd never let go.

Over the next few days, I found myself alternating between wanting to cling to Jon nonstop and resenting him. That he could so casually think about *when* he takes the girls to college, or *when* he meets their first love. When he walks them down the aisle, or when he visits them in their own homes to fix things on every vacation. I would find myself so consumed by a rage that quickly dissolved into sadness. I couldn't even look at him out of guilt. I called it what is was and pushed it out of the way. Even early on I knew that jealousy and resentment could be the end of us. They had no place here; I couldn't let them take hold of me.

I leaned more heavily on my inner circle of support to process all of this, to talk through it so I could keep moving. They were the ones who walk side by side with me, desperate to carry some of this burden, fixated on my every move, waiting to catch me and hold me up. To pull them in, I had to break the news. Breaking the news was one of the tougher parts. It came in phases, this news breaking.

I procrastinated telling my mom for longer than I intended. I pretended I was waiting until I had a full assessment of my diagnosis. Even though I knew I was really just avoiding the hurt of that call. But I now knew I was stage IV, and where the cancer had spread. I had no excuse to put it off any longer.

I stood in the hallway of my house holding my phone. The girls were at school; Jon was at work. The house was quiet. I lifted my phone to call her but had to put it down again. I closed my eyes and lifted the phone again, only to rest it on my forehead. *Make the call. Make the call*, I told myself. Until finally I opened my eyes dialed her number, more anxious with every ring of the phone.

"Helllooooo…" She always answers the phone with a long, extended hello. It made me smile.

"Hey Mom."

"Hey! How are you?" I can't dive in just yet. Not yet.

"Good. How are you?"

"Good. Oh, except this stupid sleeping stuff."

"Have a hard time sleeping last night?" Just you wait, Mama. You won't be sleeping for a while after we get off the phone today.

"I'll tell you what. It's all tied to that seven o'clock thing. Something in my head tells me I'm going to have to get up and then you know what? I can't sleep. It's just that one day at the library that I have to work early, but I know it's coming, and you know what happens then. For like three nights in a row! Because by the second night I'm so exhausted. And I get so pissed!"

She let go of a breathy laugh, and I could picture her hunched over with it.

She kept on with her story. "It does nothing but make it worse and, you know, it's not unusual, well for me, I'll wake up and say I'll bet you it's one o'clock. One o'clock!"

"That sucks, Mom."

"Oh. My. God. It's the worst. Well, somebody said that light from the iPad or computer fools your brain."

"What?"

"Yes! I forget where I was reading that. It's a psychological thing. It might have been a Facebook thing. You know how it just comes up when you're looking at the Facebook. I don't know. I don't know."

I listened, thinking about how she will crumble inward when I tell her, how her chest will hurt, how it won't let up. Maybe not ever. I let her ramble, enjoying the lightness as she jumped from topic to topic, wrapped in the warm blanket of my Mom's carefree blather about easy things.

"...That's why they said you have to take pictures. But you know...Let's get a family picture. It's like pulling freaking teeth. It's like, crazy stuff, crazy stuff. Did you get school pictures by the way?"

It had been almost five years since we were deep in the throes of cancer. We had just stopped sitting on the edge of our seats for the news at each appointment. We were almost in the clear, so close.

"... well and that's the thing. I told them forget it. For. Get. It. Because you just never know..."

I knew a break in the conversation was coming when she'd ask me about me. I was savoring these last few moments when we talked so readily about things not cancer. Time would be forever delineated by this moment. By the time before my recurrence and after. It would never be the same again.

"So. What's up with you?"

Here we go. Just say it. Softly, I said, "Well, I saw Mihailo today...."

That's all it took. She knew. Immediately, she made a steady, pained, guttural sound that was half sob, half moan. The most sorrowful noise I've ever heard. I let her be with it for a second, but then I had to keep going, to get it over with. Just say the facts. I told her about the biopsy, and the CT scan. I said the words "inflammatory carcinoma" and "metastatic."

"Okay." She was still in the sob moan.

"So far it looks like it's only in my liver. I'm going in next week for a bone scan to see if it's spread anywhere else as well."

"Ooooooooohhh, okay."

I told her, "I feel fine."

"Do you?"

"Yes. I do. I feel absolutely fine." She started moaning again then, trying to muffle it but couldn't. My heart broke for her. There are worse things than getting stage IV cancer and watching your daughter get it is one of them.

"Okay. Okay then," she said.

That was all she could really take now. "I'll call you later, okay, Mom?"

"Ooooooh. Okay, honey. I love you."

"Love you too, Mom. I'll call you tomorrow."

I had a similar conversation with Dad and Pam. My dad was speechless, only able to make random noises of shock and sorrow. Pam just barely managed to get out a very wet, "I would take it. I would take this from you." I knew she meant it.

Telling the girls was going to be even harder. I couldn't think about it before the dread was so intense it completely shut me down. I had never felt the innate maternal drive so strongly to protect my daughters from hurt. How badly I wished they didn't have to bear this. Because thirteen-year-old girls are supposed to take their mom completely for granted. That's the way it's supposed to be. But I could not imagine a world unraveling for a teenager. Couldn't imagine my girls living their lives without me. Instantly, I hoped these horrifying images would never enter their minds. Ever. It filled me with a physical ache in my stomach that made it hard to stand. I didn't want to tell them until I could spare them the pain by hiding it.

I pulled off a lightness to cancer with them during the first rodeo. They were only eight then. But now thirteen, and much more savvy. They knew Wendy, and they had talked a lot about cancer in different ways over the last five years. Jon kept encouraging me to tell the girls. It was a soft debate that consisted of Jon asking me every other day, "Do you want to tell the girls today?" and me telling him, "No, not today."

I knew he was right. I knew they deserved to know. And in a small town, there was the possibility that they could hear from someone else first. Which would be bad.

It was now into August. Jon took the girls to get their school supplies while I got more scan results to see if cancer had crept into other places. We all got home at about the same time, and I watched as my girls spread their pencils, notebooks, and folders all over the dining room table. I listened as they told me which colored supplies would be paired with each class. I watched silently and wondered how many more times I'd get to participate in this back-to-school rite of passage. I said nothing about cancer.

A few days later we were back at the cancer center talking to Mihailo about the latest test. So far, it appeared my cancer was confined to my breast and liver. After talking treatment options, Jon asked Mihailo to weigh in on when and what to tell the girls. We laid out our respective cases.

Mine was only, "Not until I'm ready."

"But I really think they should know what's happening," Jon softly insisted.

"Not," I shook my head once, staring at the floor, "until I'm ready." I looked up to Mihailo and said, "Well this is fun, Mihailo, want to hop into the middle of our marital debate?" He looked back at both of us and just waited. "Mihailo, what am I going to do if they ask me, 'When are you going to die, Mama?'" I could feel my voice start to crack. "How, What am I going to say then?"

Mihailo looked calmly right back at me. "I think you can tell them that you don't know. Because we don't know." Without a rush, but with all of his attention, he said, "I have a patient who has a very aggressive form of cancer. It was advanced, and one of the ones that doesn't usually give you much time. But he's responded really well to treatments and now, after seven years, he's probably not going to die of cancer. So, we just have to see how you respond to treatments. Until then, we just don't know."

At some point, we might know. Now we don't. But kids deal in black and white. "How do I explain this?"

"Tell them as simply as you can," said Mihailo, "when you're ready. Follow their lead for how much they're ready for now."

I thought about where to draw the line for a young teen. But I couldn't. Because I got stuck on how much I didn't want to do it at all.

Jon and I decided on the way home that we would—I would—tell the girls that evening. I was consumed by anxious anticipation about it the entire ride home, replaying my fake disregard when I broke the news five years ago. I'd have to be a much better actress. Because this wasn't the same news to break. This wasn't a friendly cancer.

When we got home, the four of us bustled around the kitchen making dinner. The girls were pleasantly present in what they thought was going to be a typical night, which only made the knot in my stomach squeeze tighter and tighter. It was a beautiful summer's evening, so we passed plates and napkins around the picnic table on our back deck, nestled in the shade from the heat of the day.

A few bites in, I decide to get it over with. "So, girls," I said, my heart pounding in my chest, "I have something to tell you." I could hardly breathe. But I *had* to sell that there was no panic here, so I put all my focus on inserting calm into each word. "I went to the doctor recently, and I found out that my cancer came back."

"Is it bad?" asked Caitlin quickly.

"It is serious," I told her slowly.

"But I mean really bad. Like the bad kind. It's not really bad, is it?"

"It is really serious. They found some again on my breast, but they also found some in my liver. There are treatments that are effective, so that's good. I'm not sure what they will be yet. We're still working that out." I was trying so hard to keep my face light. To let my body language and tone say that this was something not scary, something that didn't have to hurt.

Caitlin looked at me and nodded briefly with a thin forced smile. She wasn't buying it. She is smart as a whip that girl, but she mimicked my act. I watched her push all her emotions deep down and bury the fear below it. This was the girl who asked me nearly every day, "Mom, how are *you*?" and took the time to hear the answer; she sincerely wanted to know. When she hugged me, every day, she wrapped me up in caring until I felt completely whole. I saw all of her then, such a big heart, and wondered what mimicking my charade took away from her. Wondered if by trying to protect her from hurt, I was forcing it to fester on the inside. It almost made me break.

"Are you going to lose your hair again?" asked Lil.

"I don't think so. There are some different treatments that we could use this time. I'm not sure."

I waited for a question I didn't want to answer. I kept eating, just to add some motion to the silence. Then Lily said, "Mom, there's this pencil case I really wanted to get. That one online that I showed you..."

Jon sighed and hung his head forward. He started to say something, but I reached over and put my hand on his arm to stop him. When I looked back to Lil, I smiled and saw the girl that read *The Fault in Our Stars* last summer in a single day on a family road trip. It's a tortured story about young teens with cancer and the loss they endure. I caught a glimpse of her in the back seat just as she finished, clasping the book to her chest. She sat staring out the window and didn't say a word for 300 miles. I remembered when she tried to read the book *Ishmael*, a story of a young boy forcibly recruited to a militia in Africa. A true story and an intensely hard read about the loss of innocence when forced into the atrocities of war. She was only a few pages in when she handed it back to me, shook her head, and said only, "Too much."

This was too much. And we really should be talking about pencil cases. So, I asked her, "You mean the one with the zippers?"

"Yeah! I don't know if I should get that one though, or the one that was a little longer."

"Your new pencils might fit better in the long one," I said and took a bite of dinner. Jon was still staring down at his lap. I squeezed his arm again and smiled when he looked up at me.

Not a Hippie

Months before, I had signed up to volunteer at our local music venue, a circus tent pitched at the bottom of a ski hill for the summer. In exchange for helping to park cars, I could watch Yonder Mountain String Band and M.O.E play for free, figuring I'd catch up with whoever I found at the show after my volunteer shift. I considered skipping it. But physically, I felt absolutely fine. Since I had already done the "new-and-shocking-cancer-diagnosis" thing nearly five years ago (So close! So close to five years!), I thought that sitting around wallowing would do me no good.

But I was hollow, so numb I felt like I didn't exist. I had heard the words. I saw the scans, but it couldn't be real. With cancer back, the world turned upside down, and everything before was a long distance away. There was sound. Forms moving about. But they were all in slow motion, underwater. Nothing existed beyond four inches in front of my face. The whirlwind of cancer left me trapped in a bubble with a constant chorus of youhavecanceryouhavecancer....

It really would be more polite if everything would stop. Just give me a second to figure this out. A minute to think. But the world doesn't stop. Time relentlessly continues to pass.

I set out to push cancer aside for a few hours, and I went. It was a beautiful evening in northern Wisconsin: comfortable temperature, light breeze, a fading sun that cast the colors of sunset across the ski hill. Engulfed by a unrelenting internal haze of *I have cancer*, I grabbed my bright yellow vest and orange flag and headed down to the parking lot.

One of the other parking volunteers was a co-worker I'd known for years. After a few minutes of chitchat, he looked directly at me and said, "So, what's happening with you?" I knew exactly what he was asking from his focus and tone. Apparently, my news had made it to him, but I tried to evade cancering with a not-so-close-friend by talking about a recent trip to the lake. He interrupted and said, "No, no, what's going on with you?"

He's going to make me say it.

"Um, yeah. I, ah, just found out that my cancer returned."

He gestured for more info, "So what's the status? What are you doing?"

He's going to make me say all of it.

"Well, my breast cancer has returned in its original location, and it has spread to my liver. So that puts me at a stage IV diagnosis." I watched his shoulders sag with understanding.

"What's the treatment plan?"

Oh my God, I'm going to have to say more. "Since my cancer feeds on estrogen, and ovaries are big estrogen producers, I had them removed about a week ago." I said this the same way Mihailo first mentioned it, casually, like a side note. Mihailo had turned to the computer right after he said it, which allowed me an unseen moment of shocked terror, unable to speak, thinking, *So, we're just yanking out organs now, huh?* But I pulled it together when I let my girls know about the surgery. I told them like I was unfazed, like Mihailo did. They looked at me with the same utter horror I felt when I heard it, but played along, and nodded in silence.

The snarky part of me wanted to thank my coworker for giving me the opportunity to relive that moment. "And then I'll start hormonal therapy and chemo in a little bit."

"How long will your treatments last?" he asked.

"Until they don't work anymore," I said abruptly. *There ya go buddy. You asked until I had to say that part. Let that sink in.* We were quiet as I watched his gaze shifted from curiosity and concern to pity. I hate it when people look at me with pity. *I'm working hard not to pity myself. Don't pity me.*

Cars started pulling in then, so he started walking backwards towards his post at the entry and said, "You know what? My mom got breast cancer and decided all she was going to do was pray. And now twenty years later, she's still at it." With that he turned and started cheerfully waving his flags to direct traffic. And that's when I started to resent him. He was moving on. But I was stuck, standing in the middle of the parking lot feeling small.

The conversation tail-spinned me. What was a haze of *You have cancer* was now a heavy blanket. As more cars poured in, I turned and walked to my station to flag cars into orderly rows. Cancer was now firmly anchored in the space just two inches away from my face. I flagged a car in and said, "Hey, welcome to the Tent." *You have cancer.*

Another car pulled up. I might have even smiled briefly. "Have a good show." *You have cancer, and your liver is riddled with it right now.* I kept moving.

Once the lot was full, I took off my vest and walked towards the tent for the show. Everything at the tent was a little worn. Lengths of railroad ties lodged in the ground and backfilled with gravel served as stairs up the short, steep slope to the venue. I held on to the railing and stepped cautiously up the steps to not strain the space that used to house my ovaries. But I felt no pain at all.

I couldn't believe how unaffected I felt after the surgery. In just a few days, I was even back into doing my field work. I was sampling the coastal wetlands along Lake Superior's shoreline that summer. We'd launch a canoe at a few sites per day and paddle a short stretch to grab some water samples. The paddling and water sampling I could do but heaving the canoe up and down off the top of my minivan repeatedly was questionable. They told me not to lift anything for a few days. But I felt fine. I even called the surgeon to ask for an early release on my lifting ban. When I explained, she said, "What? You want to what? Ah, no."

My coworker assured me that he could get the canoe up on top of my van on his own. So, I did the field work anyway, but skipped the lifting. I hated it. There's an unwritten rule among field crews: you pull your own weight. Especially as a woman, I work to be the first in line for the hard stuff. But I couldn't. Instead, I watched my coworker do the heavy lifting on his own and was thankful that at least he was someone who didn't make it feel awkward or isolating. Instead, we belittled how much it sucked with a constant stream of bad humor.

At each boat landing, I'd say something like, "Hey, so I have an idea, how about I just sit here and do *nothing* while you do all the work. How'd that be?"

He'd heave the boat from my van and say, "Man, I was hoping you'd ask that. I'm trying to build some upper body strength over here." He'd set the canoe in the water and hold it extra steady for me.

I'd gingerly step into the boat and say, "I'm thinking about getting into upper management, so I'm figuring I'd just watch you work all day."

"That sounds awesome. You're gonna make a great manager."

I had my ovaries out just days before that field work, and now less than a week before this volunteering stint at the tent. I made it to the top of the stairs and looked over to the tent. It was a ridiculous thing made of blue and white-striped canvas over two stories tall. It looked animated with the series of peaks lining the mid rib at random angles. The side walls were left open so that happy hippies could spill in and out of the tent at will.

These scrubby dread heads used to be my people. In my twenties, I saw live music - jam bands, singer-songwriter types, bluegrass, jazz, you name it - a few nights a week at venues small and large. It partly defined me then, and I loved it. I'd dance for hours, engulfed in the music. I was here for a distraction, to lose myself in the band so the world would stop spinning. Just for a little bit. But instead, I felt remarkably isolated, stuck under a *You have cancer* blanket getting heavier by the second. It bullied so much I couldn't breathe.

I told myself repeatedly that I could breathe just fine. I saw some friends and pushed cancer back to six inches away from my face to say hi. We laughed and joked about the thick cloud of pot in the air, but then I had to move on. I saw another friend

I always love to talk to, but she might ask me questions. Too fragile. Couldn't handle that. I gave her a quick smile and made myself unavailable.

I told myself to not let cancer dominate. *Just let it go for one night, and let the music consume you.* But after thirty minutes or so I realized it wasn't going to happen. For the first time ever, I left the show early. I drove home slowly, thinking about past shows, about the conversation with my fellow flag bearers, and about cancer. A few blocks away from my house I saw my neighbor, a good friend. I stopped the car and rolled the window down. As soon as she leaned over to say hi, I lost it. I cried about unwanted questions and ovaries and jam bands. I sobbed about all the lighthearted hippies in the world and how I'm not one of them anymore. She stopped me there to say, "Oh, shut up, you are not a hippie."

"I was though!" I insisted.

We caught our breath and wiped our eyes. She said, "Michele, everyone is so worried about you, and no one knows what to say." We sat dumbfounded in silence and cried.

This was the landscape I was forced to navigate. The person I used to be colliding with an unfathomable reality. Engulfed in a world I couldn't imagine with a family who desperately wants and needs me. And a community that cares and wants to help. Any past insights from the first rodeo were irrelevant. The scale of this cancer was so much bigger.

No insights from the first rodeo mattered. Except one. That this was still my life. My course to set.

Finding My Way

I focused on sorting out a treatment plan in the shadows, while trying to keep the rest of our lives as routine as possible: one moment doing something as mundane as laundry, the next scheduling a brain MRI. (It hadn't spread there yet, thank God.) We tried to do normal things as much as we could to remind us that even though cancer was back, it couldn't rob us of who we are.

On a Saturday afternoon, Jon, the girls and I drove to Long Lake for the afternoon, one of our favorite local beaches. My girls are true northerners. If it's hot—and by that, I mean over 70 degrees—they are miserable to do anything but swim. We northerners are as rich in cold, clean water around here as we are shy in people. As a result, we have a handful of beaches within a five-minute drive or walk from home that we usually have to ourselves. Long Lake is one of those spots.

On the way, we listened to *This American Life,* that day's theme a series on ignorance. In one story, a young Chinese

American woman told of her grandmother's diagnosis with very advanced stage IV cancer. As soon as I heard the word "cancer" on the program I thought, *Uh oh.* I didn't do other people's cancer stories. They forced me to think about things I didn't want to think about, and I had enough cancer in my life already. I especially didn't want the girls to listen to a cancer story, in case there wasn't a happy ending.

But we left the show on. The four of us listened in silence as the young woman explained that in the Eastern philosophy of medicine, mental, emotional and physical health are completely entwined with each other. There is an old Chinese proverb that tells this well: "Two people go get a physical. One of them is healthy, and one of them has a terminal illness. The hospital gets the results mixed up. The healthy person gets a terminal prognosis and vice versa. So, then the healthy person ends up dying while the sick person ends up living."

With this mindset to wellness, lying to people about their condition was common. It spared the sick from the grief of knowing about their illness. Better to let family carry that burden so that the sick can keep a positive mental state. Out of love, the charade to hide the grandmother's illness was extensive: made up reasons to see a doctor so much, contrived explanations for all body scans, the chemo pill that was called a vitamin. Mostly, there was an insistence that all family members be happy when visiting the grandmother, even when they thought it was the last time they'd see her. *You will be sad, but you must not cry.* After the grandmother lived three years (when told she only had three months), the family was convinced that it was the lack of information, the lack of stress that allowed her to live. And it was a happy ending cancer story, a good outcome, which made us all feel a little better.

The story ended just as we reached the lake, each of us eager for the different kind of peace it offered us. Jon brought a rod and fished for bass in the wetland at the head of the lake. The girls hopped around along the sandy shoreline. They knew every inch of this beach. They were true tweeners, and the lake brought them back to the littler kid side of thirteen. They splashed each other and squealed with laughter as I snapped pictures. This was nothing shy of miraculous, since they had been refusing pictures for the last year. I finally gave up on all the threats and bribes to get a smiling picture and accepted that we'd document their mastery of the scowl. So that day, when they connected their hands in a heart as they leaned back to smile for the picture, my heart nearly exploded, and I clicked away over 200 photos.

I sat with them at the edge of the shoreline on a bench. There would be no swimming for me. They couldn't stick a needle in the skin that was inflamed with breast cancer for the biopsy, so instead they carved a circle from two spots on my breast, one along the inner section and another right on my nipple. Both were as fat as your finger and maybe a quarter inch deep. Yes, that big. Since radiated breast tissue takes so long to heal, those holes would remain wide open for many months; my swimming days were over for the summer. I could still run around the lake. The fading light of the day told me I'd better get going. But I stayed to watch the girls swim and Jon fish for a little while longer.

I thought about the value of solitude. How the stillness of this place was exactly what we all needed. It allowed us to shed the unwanted distractions of our lives. To be right here, right now. The scars on my breast tried to pull me away, but the present pulled me back each time. By watching my girls chase each other along the shoreline, with the steady plunk of a lure as Jon fished in the weeds, by a nearly imperceptible breeze that skimmed the surface of the lake. The evening brought a perfect temperature with a softness that just kissed the skin. In this stillness, I could resist the tug of unwanted thoughts and instead soak up the beauty of the present. I could feel the peace of the lake.

I had learned in the past few weeks that the eighteen-month survival estimate for inflammatory breast cancer was for initial diagnoses. Since my inflammatory diagnosis came as a recurrence, the guess on my timeline stretched. The average survival rate was more like three to five years. Later, at an appointment at Mayo for a second opinion, the doctor said, "You probably won't live to be old, but you still could have years and years, maybe even twenty?" After thinking eighteen months for a while, the possibility of three to five years, or even twenty, felt extraordinary.

What a screwed-up thing to be happy about. But after obsessing over *really* short-term plans, I felt absolutely ecstatic. I called Heather as soon as I got out of the Mayo appointment to celebrate the mere possibility of time. "Who even wants to live past 60?" she said. "That's when you start peeing your pants twice a day!" We laughed with relief.

"Maybe I'll get to be a grandma after all," I started to cry.

"Maybe you will," she cried with me.

I watched us as a family, each enjoying the lake in our own way, and thought that maybe I'd have many more summers at Long Lake. The fading light of the day was about to close my window for a run, so I pulled myself from the bench and called for my dog, "Come on, Opie."

I kept replaying the story from *This American Life* as Opie and I ran the rocky, dirt trail around the lake. In some ways, the Eastern philosophy of medicine shares similarities with the placebos of Western medicine. At some phase of nearly all clinical trials to test a new drug, participants are divided into two groups: one group gets the experimental medication and the other gets a nothing pill. No one knows who's getting what. This model shifts the question from "Does this medication work?" to "Does this medication provide benefits that are greater than taking no medication at all?" with the comparison between groups deemed the true measure of drug effectiveness.

I found this fascinating. This occurrence—that people who think, who *believe* they are taking a helpful medication can show some response—is incorporated into the established medical research system to compensate for it. It indicates the power of the mind and how much we don't know about it.

Engrossed in the contradictions and commonalities of medical approaches from different sides of the globe, I forgot to look for Opie until we reached the far side of the lake. I turned back to find him trudging along to keep up, his heavy breathing and tired gait showed the effort it took. I waited for him, "Hey buddy," and pet him gently on the head until he caught his breath. A combination of golden retriever and collie, Opie's long, thick coat of light brown and white usually bounced when he pranced around town.

People often stopped me to say, "What a beautiful dog!" And he is. Opie is the Fabio of dogs.

I smile and tell them, "Yeah, he knows."

He was not bouncing now though. I walked him to the lake to cool down. Too much of a pretty boy to fully submerge all that glorious hair, Opie waded just enough to get his belly wet and lap up some cool water. That's when I noticed his back legs shaking. A lot. Shaking like a dog who just took his last run. We walked the rest of the way back to the beach. I felt like time was passing much too quickly. Opie was fourteen; he was slowing down quickly. I hugged him, and then brought handfuls of cold water on to his back to help cool him down as he wheezed. We weren't ready for loss in our home.

I kept thinking of the radio show for days. In the treatments of western medicine, hearing I had stage IV cancer was like being told, "And now you're going to stay in this room with no doors or windows. There is no way out. No other option." It was exceptionally surreal. I heard the words, but I didn't really believe them. I thought *But I don't belong here.*

I looked for ways to relate to the Eastern medicine world view on how overall health is affected by the balance of physical, mental, and spiritual energy. How emotions influence physiology. I thought of the adrenaline response to fear that raises our heartbeat and lifts the hair on our arms. A tie between physical response from emotional stimuli that I could relate to. I dug deeper into the biochemical processes behind endorphins and chemical defense mechanisms. I wanted the magic, but I also needed hope.

Over the next few weeks, I started investigating integrative treatments in full-blown desperation to do *something*, without a clue what that something was. I devoured book after book and website after website on cancer fighting herbs and supplements. I compiled the mechanism of action, any clinical evidence of benefit or harm for each option. Curcumin has anti-cancer properties. High-dose vitamin C is the way to go. Fish oil, especially DHA, can kill cancer cells. CoQ10 does - something.

The combination of not knowing enough about the systems of the body and a loudly clicking clock made for very scattered research. At times, the severity of my diagnosis relaxed my rigor for depth of references. Desperate times call for desperate measures. I'd find myself on a website denouncing the rigors of conventional medicine alongside of a miracle cancer cure supplement on sale for only $19.99. I wondered what in the hell I was doing. The overload of information online, contradictory claims, and the onslaught of beat the odds survival stories that reeked of advertising was totally overwhelming. But then I thought about the girls' high school graduation just a few years out and placed orders for a pile of supplements. *How does it fight cancer? Not exactly sure, but I'll take it!*

And then, there were toxins. Toxins are cancer's best friend, and they're everywhere. I frantically started eliminating all toxins from my life, starting with plastics. They can offload bisphenol A, also known as BPA, a hormone-like property. I replaced all my cleaning products, studying their list of ingredients extensively before every purchase. I lined myself up for massive changes, only to oscillate immediately back over to *Does any of this matter at all?* There was too much to digest. There had to be practitioners with training that would surpass any amount of research I put into options, contradicting opinions, and interactions among treatments. I switched focus into finding them.

For that, I called Wendy.

The Wendy Diet

endy was still coaching volleyball as she received
treatment. She drove nine hours for treatment at
the Cancer Treatment Center of America in Chicago
where they specialize in evidence-based integrative treatments.
I was eager to hear about her experience there, about the kinds
of therapies they recommended. Maybe I'd incorporate a few;
maybe I'd start making the drive, so I didn't have to sort through
it all out on my own.

Mom and Heather were out for a visit, so the three of us
went to Wendy's on a late summer morning. We sat in a fine
breeze under her covered front porch. I had only briefly met
her husband, Mike, before. I'd seen him and Wendy coach the
high school and junior varsity teams. They were a fantastic pair
to watch. Wendy full of support and focus; Mike full of energy
and intensity. He's not the largest guy on the court, but he takes
up the most space with his presence. It's in the way he'll look
at you, eyes sharp and focused, brows crumpled. His command

and volume. He makes you feel like you're in the hot seat, like you should really pay attention. And then he'll smile, and his whole face changes; he positively glows. The players strove for that smile.

Chelsea, one of their daughters, joined us as well. I had never met Chelsea, but a cancer introduction cuts right through all the formalities. "Sorry, sometimes I get weepy," she said when she hugged me. Chelsea and her sisters worked in the details, so that Wendy could focus on her wellness. Chelsea had pulled together a pile of resources for me, books and DVDs, with all the breast cancer content flagged for me.

We spent hours there that morning. Their approach was to hit cancer with everything they could, conventional and integrative treatments combined. Diet adjustments intend to starve cancer by limiting simple sugars and loading up on cancer-fighting foods that boost the immune system.

"Berries are good," said Wendy, reaching for a couple from the bowl they had out on the table.

"Lots of antioxidants in them," said Chelsea. I grabbed a few strawberries.

"No simple carbohydrates. No bread. No potatoes or white rice," Wendy told me.

"But brown rice is okay," said Chelsea.

Mike interrupted, "You don't want that brown rice though." He looked disgusted.

Chelsea waved a fly away from the berries and covered them with a paper towel. "It's fine. Brown rice has a lower glycemic index than white. It won't spike your blood sugar as much. You just have to cook it a little longer."

"Huh! It doesn't cook at all. On the stove for over an hour and it's still hard." He scowled at the thought of it. I tried not to smile because he seemed pretty pissed off about brown rice.

"Focus on veggies, especially cruciferous ones." Chelsea continued. "Broccoli, cauliflower, cabbage, Brussel sprouts. They all have cancer-fighting properties."

"What about meat?" I asked. "I keep on reading about going vegan."

"Mostly veggies. But we'll do some chicken, only organic. Sometimes fish, but we avoid anything that might carry metals. Like tuna, swordfish, old lake trout," said Chelsea. Consistent with the data I'd seen. This was affirming.

"Lemon is good." Wendy said. "We put lemon in water all the time."

"Citrus is a good detoxifier of the liver," explained Chelsea. I took a sip of my lemony water.

I considered the reality of eating this way. The restrictions were so severe, there wasn't much left to eat. "You must eat a lot of veggies to get enough food in a day."

"Juicing. We do a lot of juicing. The goal is to get down four 16-ounce veggie drinks a day. But yeah, Mom eats a bunch of small meals all day long. She's still dropping weight though."

Wendy sat a little taller, "My weight is fine." She clearly had dropped a lot of weight in the past year. Maybe 40 pounds.

Mike ratted her out though. "She tried to get on the scale with weights in her bag at the last appointment." He was not happy about this, but there was a faint grin at the deviousness of it. Wendy stared straight ahead, looking at none of them, chin held high.

Mike continued, "I think this stuff works though. The tumors shrinking, I think this is helping. But the regular doctors don't even think about all this other stuff. We were at an appointment last month and, they offered her a donut." He shook his head. But then he looked at me hard and said, "You take the time to take care of yourself. Right now, it's all about you." His intense gaze made me feel like he'd be watching and would have something to say if he saw a lack of self-care put first. I was definitely going to make it all about me. Yessir.

We talked about food and supplements. Cannabis and mushrooms. Amounts, sources, and concentrations. The importance of exercise and meditation. I thought that there would be a singular, defined prescription to follow in the integrative cancer treatment world, but I realized there wasn't. They put together their systems of treatments by researching the same way I had. There wasn't one path in the integrative medicine route. I'd have to figure this out on my own, no avoiding the conjecture, lack of clarity and contradictions.

What struck me most was the way they all talked to each other. They were months ahead of us on the stage IV road, and I could feel how that time made space for even more love. My mom, sister, and I were still in shock, dumbfounded. We were keeping all the cancer talk bound up on the inside, since it felt like letting the words out would make it real. But it was real, and letting the cancer chatter out relieved some of the pressure. Being around Wendy and her family made me realize that we could start talking about it, that the future would be full of talking about it. Forever.

Tango Interlude 2

She's become accustomed to the struggle it is to get to the roof, the stairs of an Escher painting that might never end. At first, she holds on to the railing out of convenience, but by the next landing, she's practically pulling herself up the stairs. She stops for a moment to catch her breath, wondering how she will Tango when just getting there takes all she has. The frustration of it pisses her off, and she stomps the rest of the way to the roof.

She plows right through the frosted glass door, and practically runs into him, sitting in that same metal chair. He hardly responds, tying his shoes like always. He looks so worn, resigned. It shames her that his fatigue irritates her, but she can't help it. She is sick of fatigue. She walks past him to the edge of the roof to take a deep breath in the dark of night for another moment, while the stars are still visible. She looks over to the tallest of the skyscrapers, the only other one that is on par with theirs. She refuses to look down. As if it heard her anyway, light spills around the base of the building, climbing up the backside as fast as an elevator. Impossible for her to ignore anymore. By the time he's finished tying his shoes, the moon has reached the penthouse suite and the light of it explodes from the top, blindingly bright, as wide as the building from which it erupted. The moon has arrived.

He stands up from the metal chair and looks to her. She is focused, amped up as she struts past him to move the chair out of the way. When she turns back towards him, she is in the dance, and he is ready. They walk to each other with intention, both embodying the dance's famous forwardness. Their upper bodies remain totally still, all bounce removed by the shocks of their legs. Each footfall is articulated with different degrees of staccato. They stall, holding each step until the last possible moment in a dramatic, march-like approach to each other. It is all familiar now.

They have learned the language of this dance very well, its subtle vocabulary told in motion. She remembers when he would look to read the surface of her. How he would study her from his own uncertainty. She smiles at the memory, knowing the pure intention of that effort, remembers her own attempts at the same.

How silly. To think your way through Tango. Hollow and incomplete. It does no good. It took years to feel emotion transferred through the pressure and force of touch, through compression and resistance, in the structure of their frames. Their dance is a leap between islands of balance, standing on one foot until it can no longer support you, then trusting, hoping, that the next landing will hold. They dance Tango over and over and over until movement of hand and arm, of forward and backward steps, just happens without hesitation.

It is a different dance now though. They need more space for the sweeping steps of this Tango. The size of the dance floor has grown to a broad, grand stage. The moves are not as prescribed; they lack a defined path. A foundation remains but intuition and experimentation claim more now. It's unsettling enough to inadvertently up the tempo. They cross the floor in that rushed pace scouring every inch for a lost attempt. They focus on the dance when they are dancing, and they obsess on developing the whole of it when they are not. They just need to know that they've done everything they could.

They are so tired. From the dance, but also from the consuming hunger of the moon. So bright, relentless, draining. They are a mixture of exhaustion and conviction, uncertainty and fire. They keep dancing despite the constant chaos spiraling around them.

She is uneasy tonight, a caged animal. He can feel it. She is too distracted to even let him catch her eye. She breaks free of him and begins to spin. He expects her back after a twirl or two, but she keeps spinning. Arms above her head now and whirling faster, headed right towards the moon. He watches, mesmerized, and slightly concerned. She hasn't Tangoed like this before. He waits, but she keeps going until it dawns on him. She doesn't realize. But he does, and he rushes to her. By the time he grabs her by the waist, they are on the brink of the rooftop. She grabs him back just as hard, and they stand breathing heavily under the glower of the moon.

She throws his hands off her and roars at the moon with a deafening ferocity. She is a dragon, Nazgul, demon, Viking, warrior. She is leaning so far into her rage that he worries she might fly off the edge. She growls at it again, harder this time with a guttural scream so filled with fury the people in the street below can feel her pain on the back of their necks. Some of them shutter and stay focused on whatever else they were doing. A handful stop instantly and hurry into the skyscraper from which her cries came.

The moon won't acquiesce that easily though. It glows back just as bright with an indifference that discards them as futile. But then the wind off the water picks up, engulfing them in the salty air. A gust of it pushes them back from the edge, and they feel the temperature drop. The misty gusts shift to a barrage of icy pellets. They hate it but stand tall anyway. They stare back at the moon in a refusal of defeat. Neither side will yield tonight.

No Right Answers

I was settling into a stage IV cancering groove. With my conventional treatments set, I started looking for more support with integrative treatments. I wasn't comfortable going completely alternative—meaning dropping the conventional stuff entirely—but did want to integrate some additional therapies to boost my odds. I had already changed my diet drastically and added in a few supplements, but I was self-prescribing quantities. I had no idea what I was doing. I looked for some different options.

Take 1: The Bankruptcy Route

A friend sent me a link to a fascinating webinar with MDs discussing integrative approaches to fighting cancer. They presented simplified imagery of cancer as a big ball of cells. Conventional cancer treatments destroy 80 percent of those cells very well. But the cells that are resistant, they're the wily ones. They morph and grow until they surface again even nastier than the original bundle. The webinar presenters showed research results on nutritional and botanical supplements that worked on the stubborn cells of that cancer ball.

Yes! This was what I wanted: a research-based combo of conventional and alternative approaches that would up my odds. The cancer center from the webinar was in Chicago, a 9-hour drive, which was less than convenient but doable. I called the next day and learned that treatment there would cost $30,000 per year, most of which to cover a specialized blood test twice per year. Since my insurance didn't cover treatment out of state, I'd have to cover that fee out of pocket.

How much is your life worth? Or rather, how much is the possibility of living longer worth?

I considered pulling money from my retirement account. But if the treatments actually worked, how many years could I afford until I was out of money, leaving my family with no mom and no savings. I decided to keep that option in my back pocket and look for something else.

I scoured the web for integrative practitioners within four hours of home. I sent emails and made dozens of phone calls to intuit the legitimacy of each clinic by drilling them about their approach, credentials, and success rate. It was kind of like high-stakes, online dating. I'd never done that either. But I realized I was going to end up "single" forever looking for perfection if I didn't just give one of them a try.

Take 2: The Hipster with Bling

I found a clinic a few hours south that had the word "research" all over its website. After a mildly reassuring phone call, I set up an appointment with Dr. Jane. Jon and I filled the drive with hopeful curiosity, preparing a list of questions and imagining the mind-blowing new treatments Dr. Jane would offer up. All my doctors' visits to date had been within the only system I had known: the conventional system of Western medicine that I trusted to cure me of any sickness.

But that system was going to fail me. It prepared me for failure every time it said, "Stage IV," leaving me to question that system. Is there ever only one grand truth? Isn't it simply arrogance to claim a singular course of treatment as the only viable option? There were certainly perspectives of value that worked outside of western conventional medicine.

I'm so freaking clever. I can rationalize myself into anything.

Or maybe I'm just becoming more enlightened. I had no idea.

Around lunchtime, we made it to Dr. Jane's clinic, a single-story brick building hard to distinguish from the neighboring homes in upper middle-class suburbia. A receptionist with black hair dyed hot pink offered us hot tea: organic lemon and ginger tea. Real ceramic mugs, no plastic. Good sign.

As we settled in with cups of tea, Jon leaned over and whispered, "There are a lot of old people in here."

"Yeah, it's usually a bunch of old people and me in the waiting room." I've always liked older people, and now I was even better able to relate to talking about medications, side effects, and symptoms. I got it. Inside each one of those old folks was a younger person saying, "Can you believe this? I take all these funny-sounding meds, and my body just doesn't work like it used to."

"I can't believe it either," I wanted to say to them. "Tell me more."

Dr. Jane came out to gather us from the waiting room. She was a slight woman, maybe her late 50's, her chin-length bob of grey hair framed a kind face. As we followed her to the exam room, I noticed her funky, purple patterned leggings and high black boots. Apparently alternative medicine practitioners are also kind of hip.

I was eager to hear about new treatments, so I rushed through my cancer history when we got to the exam room. I felt Jon's hand on my back as I did, seemingly looking more for comfort than giving it. I was so accustomed to the spiel that I was unaffected. Jon didn't have to hear this as often. I don't think he liked it.

Dr. Jane recommended taking intravenous alpha lipoic acid and ozone, both of which could be administered right there in their office. *Here we go,* I thought. *Let's dig into this.*

I asked what these compounds were and how they would work.

"They support the liver," she said, nodding slightly with affirmation, "and you'll need that."

"How would they support my liver?"

"They hold the liver up and help rebuild it," she said, cupping her hands in front of herself, as if she was holding my liver right there.

Whenever I talked through my options with Mihailo, I'd ask a billion questions. Most of which he'd answer just after saying, "Good question," and then described how a healthy system functions, how cancer interfered, how a medication interrupted cancer's effort and the range of what was achievable. I was looking for a similar description.

I asked Dr. Jane again how these treatments worked, but she said basically the same thing: nothing. I considered pressing the question, but it seemed she didn't have any more to offer. Was the treatment not well vetted? Or was it just her delivery? I'd have to learn more about alpha lipoic acid and ozone elsewhere.

I showed her the mushroom tincture I took daily. Wendy used the tincture as well until her team examined it under a microscope and found a mold growing in it. I asked Dr. Jane if they did any testing like that there.

"No," she said. "Although, there is another way to look into that." She stood and reached for something on the shelf above my head. Then she held it in front of me, a decorative crystal, wrapped in metal embellishments. It was attached to a chain about ten inches long with a shiny, blue marble on the end.

"Relax your shoulder, and keep your elbow in with your wrist relaxed," she demonstrated letting the charm dangle from her hand. "Now pick a way for yes and one for no. Let's say a circle for yes. And back and forth for no. It's important to be very clear about which is which. Then you ask a question—it has to be a very clear yes or no question—and the energy will move the chain with the right answer."

Jon and I just sat there. I couldn't believe it.

"Let's try it," she continued. "Is my name Jane?" We all stared at the blue bead as it started to move in a circle. "See! It works! Is my name Tom?" The bead shifted to a back and forth motion. "I'm not even moving this," she assured us. I worked hard to keep my face expressionless. But I'm pretty sure my mouth was hanging open by then. I kinda wondered if she was joking.

"You'll have to practice for a while to get the energy right. Start with simple things. If you have a brown couch, ask 'Is the couch brown?' Stuff like that. But then you could ask if the tincture is right for you and the charm will tell you."

No, not joking. She was really serious about this.

"You can use anything that swings," she said. "Even a paper clip and some dental floss."

I sat staring at her blankly. Because the only thing I could think to say was, "Are you freaking kidding me?" But that would be rude. Some may look to crystal twirling to guide their decisions about treatments. Whatever works for you. But this was not my gig.

I changed the subject and asked about testing for virus panels, toxins, heavy metals, and hormones. These were all big in the online alternative cancer treatment world.

Jane confirmed they did that kind of testing, but then just nodded and sat there silently.

I'm pulling freaking teeth here, lady! I calmly said, "So do you have any more info about those tests?"

Jane nodded and started digging around for the test kits in a cabinet across the room. When she was hidden by cabinet door, Jon and I made eye contact. He first opened his eyes wide then immediately furrowed his brow. After fifteen years together, a glance is all it takes. I returned the same look briefly and then quickly shook my head *No*.

Jane left the room to make copies of the test descriptions for us. As soon as she closed the door, Jon said, "I'm going to say something."

"Don't say something."

"I have to say something," he insisted.

"Don't."

"The crystal," Jon shook his head with astonishment. "Did she really just say to fight cancer with a paper clip and some floss? What the hell?" I started to laugh but quickly capped it or I wouldn't be able to stop. "I feel like what we need is someone who can be a part of our team and make solid recommendations on what we can do."

"We're not going to get that here, honey," I said right as Dr. Jane walked back into the room.

I moved on to diet. Can I eat beets, or do they have too much sugar? Is venison okay? Jane provided her insights as she had them, but there were a lot of "I don't know" answers. I appreciated her honesty. I asked her about Sriracha. Perfect on a hard-boiled egg, but is that small amount of cane sugar (only one gram per teaspoon) too much?

"I don't know," Dr Jane said. "But you could try this. Take the bottle of Sriracha and hold it too your chest. Ask if it is okay for you. If it is not, you'll be pushed forward on to your face, like you're getting shoved to the ground." She lurched a few times to really hammer it home. "If it's okay, you'll be able to stand tall." She sat back and relaxed her shoulders.

I was speechless. I knew if I even cracked a smile I would dissolve into hysterical laughter. Laughing fever! Highly contagious! But it's not okay to laugh at people. I didn't dare look at Jon. I bit my lip. I worked hard to keep my face expressionless.

"Well, that's something to think about," I said. I looked down at the rest of my list of questions and decided to skip them. We thanked her for her exceptionally valuable time and left.

Take 3: The Seemingly Informed Red Squirrel

A trusted friend suggested another integrative practitioner only a few hours south, Dr. Peterson, a chiropractor who specialized in researching whole body treatments to create an inhospitable environment for cancer. I called to learn more, and he jumped right into a frantic, rapid fire outpouring of every supplement and physiological modification he'd researched over the years. He talked about changes in body chemistry as a result of cellular destruction. He talked about endothelial cells and something about free radicals and the endocrine system. Cellular processes and mechanics.

The guy was like a red squirrel, bouncing from topic to topic so quickly I couldn't follow at all. Which gave me a small hesitancy. I'd worked with researchers who, guarded by ego, show off their expertise by ensuring it's inaccessible, which often hides an incomplete understanding of the topic. I wasn't sure where he fell on that spectrum. But he did seem knowledgeable, and his foundation of practice based on clinical trial data and research appealed. I mean at least he was offering better explanations than "…to support the liver." We decided to give it a go.

Jon and I reached his clinic at 7 a.m. It was a worn-looking grey building with a flat roof that sagged a bit in the middle. I hoped that what the place lacked in stature it would make up for in substance.

The receptionist, Betty, greeted us as we walked in. "Doc's not here yet. Should be soon though," and right on cue, Dr. Peterson burst through the door like he was escaping something from outside. He hustled right by us without saying a word and rushed around behind partitions in the office doing, I have no idea what. We waited.

After a few minutes, Betty said, "Okay, you can come on back now. Did you bring that urine sample?" Testing urine was a key component of his approach, because testing urine would discern how my body was processing essential constituents, not just what was floating around in my blood stream. I handed her a bag with a container of my sample as we followed her to the exam room.

"Exam room" was a generous description; it was really more of a closet. Way too small for the four of us. A table/bed filled most of the space, with just enough room for a small desk buried under papers and folders stacked at least two feet high. I went to sit in the hard chair by the desk, but Betty stopped me.

"You come on over here. Take your shoes off and lie down on the exam table here," she said as she shuffled out of view. Dr. Peterson stepped forward while pulling small sticky squares off a plastic sheet and put two of them on one of my feet and another two on my hand.

"Don't worry, the shock will only hurt a little bit." I looked at him. "Kidding," he said with a smile. He continued fiddling with the electronics hooked up to the cables and pads. In his rapid fire chattering he explained how Navy SEALS use this device to measure the body's composition in preparation for deep sea diving. "You've heard of the BMI, right? This provides so much more than that. The percent of your body weight that is fat, visceral fat, water and bone. How much of that water is intra or extra-cellular." After about ten seconds, he pulled the pads from my hands and feet.

I took a seat in the chair next to the desk as Betty brought in a platter full of plastic pipettes and small trays with rows of small, circular depressions. There were bottles of powders and liquids, and small empty cups that could have been shot glasses.

"Here," said Dr. Peterson as he handed me one of those little cups full of liquid. "Swish this around in your mouth." I hesitated, and he said, "Lemon juice. Yep, just swish and then swallow." I obeyed, and he handed me a small strip of yellow paper. "Now wet this with your saliva. Not too much."

I handed him the paper, now green, and he lined it up with a matching green on a colorimetric scale that would indicate a reading. "I'm testing your body's ability to buffer. Lemon juice is acidic, so it will naturally drop your pH. Now we'll measure it again every minute and see how well you can bounce back up to an alkaline state. Cancer can't survive in an alkaline state. Here, take another one of these." I wet the next strip, and he briefly held it up to the color chart and scribbled down another number.

Betty came back in then with the small, light yellow container of my pee.

"Look at that!" he exclaimed. "You can tell already that you're going to be okay. Just look at how light that is! You should see what some people come in here with. Dark orange. Here, take another one of these strips for pH."

Jon and I looked at each other. Pee color seemed a gross oversimplification of my likely outcome. What about dehydration? Chemo meds? Did I just eat asparagus? I was hoping he wasn't going to pull out a crystal.

He opened the urine sample and started putting drops of my pee into the sampling tray: a few drops there, ten in the next one, then just one drop in that divot next to it. Then he used the other pipettes to mix in other chemicals in quick succession. Some turned black. Others fizzed up and turned white. Others did very little as far as I could tell. I peppered him with questions as he mixed drops of urine and chemicals, furiously trying to understand what this all meant.

He had me put another liquid in my mouth and then spit it out. "Taste anything?" he asked.

"Nope."

"You can't even taste the zinc because your body is so full of a toxic load of metals you're carrying. Can't absorb any more." He wrote some more numbers in my chart. *Did swishing liquid zinc actually determine my metal load?* I asked myself, thinking about what it takes to build trust. Credentials help. A demonstrated knowledge of subject matter helps. Are communication skills synonymous with competence? I came here for something outside of what I knew. For something extra that would help me get out of this locked room of stage IV cancer that I didn't belong in. But was I letting my desperation for that crack get in the way of my judgement? I tried to stay open without forming an opinion just yet.

"This is a whole-body treatment," he explained. "You need to heal your mind as well." Dr. Peterson instructed me to eliminate stress and raise my endorphins. "If you blow up and loose it, even just from road rage, your body chemistry will weaken your immune system for at least eight hours. Focus on things that make you happy. Whether that's petting your dog or holding your husband's hand. your body chemistry is affected by everything."

I was to be a peaceful, zen-ed out cancer patient. With teenage daughters.

"Look up T-cells killing cancer cells online," he told me. "And visualize your T-cells multiplying and killing cancer every night."

After about 45 minutes of furiously testing saliva and urine, he scribbled out a list of supplements for me, and then rushed out the door to his next appointment. I left with a giant box full of randomly sized pills and powders in something in between complete disbelief in this nonsense and hope.

When we got home, I unpacked all the tubs and bottles on my kitchen counter and stood studying them, wondering if the red squirrel was to be trusted. Wondering if I was burning money. Wondering how long he followed up with the patients he'd saved from cancer so far. "Do I do this?" I asked Jon.

"Well, we bought it all," he said.

"Yeah but look at all this. How am I going to take all of this?"

"You'll figure it out, honey," Jon gave me a hug and a kiss on the top of my head. "This is what you wanted, right? Someone who seems really well informed."

"Is he legit though, that's my question."

"What do you think?"

I considered this. Maybe you have to be like a red squirrel to find, evaluate, and weed through all the competing or contradictory information. And unlike Dr. Jane, he had confident answers for his prescriptions based on physiological body processes, even though I couldn't understand them. But he made ridding myself of cancer sound so simple. Which made me skeptical, because cancer is not easy, or predictable.

I didn't know. I realized I wasn't going to know. But I'd rather take action with uncertainty than do nothing. And I had to be open to things outside the norm to integrate the alternative approach into my conventional one. "I think it's worth a try."

Every Day I Get It

A few weeks after my appointment with Dr. Peterson I had a new routine with all my supplements. It was a typical morning in early spring. Daylight had started to filter into our bedroom. I nudged Jon so that I could lay my head on his chest. I nestled in closer, and he wrapped me up in him. We fit together perfectly and rested there delaying the start of the day. After about ten minutes, Jon got out of bed while I procrastinated letting the daily whirlwind begin. The frantic cyclone of cancer treatments all day long started before I even got dressed. I applied a topical CBD salve all over my breast, towards my chest where the lymph nodes were enlarged, and back into my arm pit area as well. Mihailo was impressed with the rapid improvement of this area when we started treatment. A result I attributed at least in part to the CBD salve. I applied it every day and night. I did not skip an application ever.

I made it downstairs to the kitchen and started my routine with a serving of Essiac tea. Since it was most effective on an empty stomach, I poured myself two ounces and topped it off with a splash of water, so it only faintly tasted of dirt before I chugged it down.

I set the tea kettle on the stove then pulled a heap of fruits and veggies from the fridge. My salad would include cabbage (it breaks down estrogen in the liver), romaine lettuce, watercress and broccoli (Cruciferous veggies are especially cancer fighting; I ate them every meal.), carrots, red pepper, and tomato. I strove for a colorful salad to mix up all the nutritional benefits, but also because I needed to like my meals to stick with this diet.

I was chopping my salad veggies when Lil came in. Lil was awake before the rest of us. She set two alarms. The first at 6:45, the second alarm ten minutes later with a ring tone she didn't like to make sure she was up before 7:00. I did not teach her this. Sometimes I wonder who the parent is here.

"G'morning, Bug," I said without looking up from the veggie pile I was loading into a square Tupperware container—glass not plastic. She grunted in response as she started slathering jelly on a tortilla. She left the knife on the counter and a big glob of jelly with it.

"Could you put that knife in the sink please?" I asked her. She sighed with irritation as she dumped the knife into the sink and started walking out of the room. I worked to take the irritation out of my voice again as I said, "and wipe up that jelly."

"I *know*, Mom," she said, dripping with teenage exasperation. These were her favorite words lately. She said 'I know' about four times a day. *If 'you know' maybe you could stop doing this every stinking day!* I thought.

My frustration dissolved almost immediately, overpowered by recognizing that I was here to experience being her parent. I loved seeing Lily become more independent and self-sufficient every day. I heard a description recently that parents of teenagers are like the walls of a swimming pool. We are the solid thing that our kids get to push off of. They tread for a while as they build the strength to swim away. But for those teen years, they still need that wall to come back to. And I was grateful that I was here to be that wall. I loved the work of trying to get Lily to allow herself to stay connected to us even as she needed to start swimming in her own direction. I loved that I knew that she needed me to take the intensity out of my tone with her, because, poor kid, she's hard enough on herself already.

No doubt still annoyed that I mentioned the jelly glob, Lil hustled out of the kitchen as Jon walked in. "What time is it?"

I looked up at the stove clock, "7:20."

"Is Caitlin up?"

"Probably not."

He hollered up the stairs, "CaitLIN!"

She hollered back with equal irritation, "WHAT!" She was in a sleepy haze, annoyed that she was unfairly being woken up, again.

"Caitlin get up, or your iPod is mine this evening!" We heard her throw her covers back and stomp toward the bathroom.

The tea kettle whistled, and I poured a tablespoon of hot water into a mug with matcha, a green tea powder that contained a cancer fighter called ECGC. I prepared one matcha for the morning and another two to three cups of steeped green tea throughout the day.

I moved on to smoothies: three a day. "So, what do you have going on today?" I asked Jon.

"Well, I have a showing at 10:00...." He started as I dumped a handful of spinach into the blender. I was hardly listening but said, "Uh huh" at the appropriate pauses as I added a half of a green apple (green apples have less sugar than other varieties), a quarter of a lemon (good detoxifiers), and ginger (anti-inflammatory) into the blender. "... and then this afternoon..."

"Hold on a sec," I said as I started the blender. I loved this blender. It attacked carrots or almonds or kale with ferocity and turned them into a smooth juice with ease. Chewing my fruit and veggie drinks was not sustainable. But emulsifying solids to liquids turned out to be ridiculously loud. We all became accustomed to one-minute pauses in conversation. I hit the green smoothie setting, and let it rip. While it screamed away, I started pulling out veggies for smoothie two: kale (more cruciferous veggies!), frozen strawberries and blueberries (full of antioxidants, but only a few to keep the sugar down).

When the blender finished, Jon continued, "... I'm meeting with some folks at 4:00 to write an offer."

"There's a volleyball game tonight," I told him, knowing he'd have a tight window to make it to the game.

"What?"

"It's a home game. You should make it in time for the start." Caitlin trudged in then and sat at the kitchen table, still only half awake.

"Hey, Caitie Ray," I said.

"My name," she corrected me, "is Caitlin."

"I know, honey, I named you. Are you going to get some breakfast?"

She grunted.

"Don't you have a volleyball game tonight?" I knew this would wake her up.

"Oh yeah," she sat up.

"Who are you playing?"

"We're playing South Shore," Lily said as she popped back in to grab her pre-made lunch from the fridge. "They took second in the tournament last week, so it should be a good game," she said over her shoulder as she walked out again. I followed her to grab a few bags for my lunch from the hallway closet. I learned from unfortunate experience to use the canvas bags that were strong enough to hold all the mason jars full of liquids.

"Caitlin, get some breakfast, honey," I told her as I walked back into the kitchen. This time I hit the frozen drink setting for smoothie number two. The blender took command of the kitchen again as I prepped smoothie three: almond milk and a scoop of powdered organic greens, including reiki mushrooms. I had no chance of finding real, raw reiki mushrooms in northern Wisconsin. But for only $1.53 a serving, this powder gave me a full daily dose. Just as I finished putting the lid on smoothie three, I heard the front door close.

"Did Lily just leave?" asked Jon.

"Yep," I told him.

He got up and opened the front door to call down the street. "Hey Lil, I think you forgot something."

"Da-aaad. I'm going to be late," I heard her complain, enjoying the attention at the same time.

"Hey," he was half laughing now with his arms stretched wide, "Don't leave without saying goodbye. Come here and give me a hug."

I called out from the kitchen. "We'll be up at the school at 5:30ish, Lil."

"Are you going to drive to the game?" she asked, stepped out of her hug with Jon.

"Nope, won't be home in time."

"Okay," she said and turned to leave again. "But you'll be there for the game?"

"Wouldn't miss it." I told her, hugging her as well. "Have a good day, Lil. Work hard. Have fun. Be nice to someone who needs it."

"I know. You always say that. Why do you say that *every* day?"

"Because *every* day you should do those things. Love you, honey."

"Love you too," as she started down the street.

There were a lot more *Love yous* since cancer returned. My recognition and appreciation of a common morning was palpable. I did not take it for granted, not for a minute. I said *love you* every time I realized the gift of the four of us being together. I said it every time I left the room from one of those three. They quickly picked up on it as well. Maybe as habit, but maybe because we all felt it just a little more deeply.

When I got back to the kitchen, Caitlin was still sitting there. "Caitlin, will you please hurry up!" I enunciated every syllable to make my point. I finished packing my bags with brazil nuts (loaded with selenium, a breast cancer fighter) and jar of chaga tea and added some almond milk (no dairy - it contains a hormone that was tied to promoting tumor growth).

She slowly shuffled up the stairs. I started filling a half gallon mason jar with tap water and a slice of lemon. I didn't drink chlorine - ties to breast cancer. Our tap water was groundwater sourced and not chlorinated, with no observable amounts of arsenic or other heavy metals. I'd checked the city's monthly testing records. The water was chlorinated where I worked just fifteen minutes away, so I brought all of my water with me for the day.

I pulled out my pill container and started swallowing them two or three at a time. I catalogued their intended benefits as I swallowed them and said a little prayer with each one. The tiny little mustard colored one was letrozole, which works to lower estrogen levels. *Please keep me alive little pill.* I-brance was the orange and brown encapsulated chemo pill. Its job was to make the letrozole work longer. *Go do your thing but take it easy on me.* Vitamin D, calcium, curcumin, CoQ10. *Help my liver out, all of you.*

And now the grand finale. The fish oil. Peterson was very particular about the brand and delivery method of fish oil. No pill would do. It had to be the actual oil to maximize absorption. I thought about using one of the measuring spoons at first, but it seemed like too much slurping would be needed from the deep shape of the teaspoon. Instead, I went for a regular spoon from the cutlery drawer. I filled it carefully with the thin clear oil and poured it hesitantly into my mouth.

The strength of its fishy flavor was shocking, and it made me gag immediately. I've handled a lot of fish in my career. This tasted like slowly rotting soft bodied fish that have been stuck in a gill net overnight. I saw their milky white eyes and shedding scales as I swallowed it down with hopes of muting the taste. No luck. Those putrid fish were still floating around in my mouth.

I took a swig of water to wash it down, but that just spread the taste around my entire mouth until I was inside of those rotting fish, covered in their sticky slime. It was brutally revolting. I started to laugh—the laughter of panic—when I thought about taking one teaspoon of this nastiness per day. The. Most. Disgusting. Thing. I. Have. Ever. Tasted.

The trick, I soon learned out of desperation, was to pour it in the very back of my throat, to avoid my tongue all together, and chase it with vitamin C powder. Phew.

I grabbed a bottle of sriracha and a couple of hard-boiled eggs so the pill/fish oil combo wouldn't upset my stomach. After holding the Sriracha to my chest for a moment and left still standing, I figured I was safe drizzling some on there. As I was cracking the shell, Caitlin walked in and asked, "Mom, can you drive me?" She asked me this nearly every day, and 95 percent of the time I said no. But it was that five percent that kept her asking. I looked at the clock. School was only three blocks away, and she could make it on time if she hurried. But I was feeling generous that morning.

"Grab your backpack," I told her.

"Yes!" she said and sprung down the hallway.

I was a bag lady. The amount of food and liquids I brought to work each day was ridiculous. As I hauled my bags of food and liquids to the car, Jon brought the dog back in the house.

"Bye, honey," I gave him a kiss on the cheek.

"Is Caitlin gone yet?"

"I'm driving her."

"What? She can walk! It's only a few blocks."

"I know. I'm driving her."

"Michele, if you keep bailing her out every time she's late, she'll have no reason to be on time."

"True. I'm driving her today though. See you tonight. Love you."

It used to make me crazy when Jon would push for his way like it was an absolute truth. When every bit of my being called to do things one way and he derailed it with adamancy, it would make my blood boil. In those early years, I used to give in. But

not as much now. Now I saw the waxing and waning, the ebb
and flow of our parenting with much more tolerance, even with
appreciation. Our family sat at the fulcrum of this pendulum,
and we were all better off for it. The girls benefited from the
things that Jon held them accountable to, and just as much for
the things I let slide. I was the good cop. He was the bad cop.
Until we needed to switch those roles, and then we did.

"Bye, Dad!" Caitlin was so excited that she was getting a ride
she practically floated to the car. She gave him a quick squeeze
and said, "Love you!" with her backpack half slung over her
shoulder. I stopped her when I saw that she was wearing a short
sleeve shirt and no jacket. It was just above freezing. "Hold on,
kiddo. Go find your jacket."

"Oh, I'm good," she tried to get past me.

"Nope. Go find your jacket. I'm leaving in two minutes, with
or without you, and only if you have your jacket." She sighed
and turned to go find her jacket. Jon and I looked at each other,
smiled slightly, and shook our heads.

Caitlin joined me two minutes and thirty seconds later. She
started flipping through radio stations as we headed to the high
school. "Oh wait, Mom," she said. "I forgot that permission slip
you signed for me. Can you write me out a new one?"

"Caitlin!"

"I know! Sorry, I just forgot," she started digging in her
backpack for a pen and scrap of paper.

"Honey, you need to work on this," I told her as I scribbled
my permission.

"I will. Thanks, Mom!" She snagged the note and headed
for the door.

"Work hard today, Caitlin." I called after her. "Have fun."

She looked back to me to say, "and be nice to someone who
needs it."

"That's my girl," I told her. She looked over her shoulder with a smile.

I watched her enter the building with a few other just-in-time stragglers, thinking about how much I loved being here to parent that kid. I loved that I knew that she was still hard to wake at 13-years-old. I loved the work of trying to help her become more accountable. I loved that I knew I needed to put more intensity into the way I talked with her, to get through her stubborn barrier. Poor kid. For every word of criticism, I worked to give her three of praise. She bloomed like a flower under the light of that praise. And it's easy for me to have patience for something as little as a sleepy start, being too late to grab a jacket, or a forgotten permission slip, because I was that kid. I still am. When it comes to the things that really matter, the gifts of the heart like compassion and empathy, she is rock solid. I have so much to learn from her.

As I started to drive away, I felt the whirlwind of the morning fizzle, and I was filled with an overwhelming sense of peace and gratitude. Amidst the chaos, the mess, the hollering, the frustration, I *loved* all of this. Because I was here to experience it.

And so we walked side by side: the Michele that has cancer and the Michele that has a life outside of it, in spite of it. Cancer no longer bullied in that space right in front of my face. It kept trying, and I pushed it back by focusing on the present. I did not think of the future. I stayed firmly rooted in right now. Cancer sat on my shoulder; sometimes it even slept. Always there, but it didn't dominate. It was belittled by the intense and fierce commitment I had to all things not cancer. To my girls. To Jon. To myself. Maybe cancer will become more dominant again someday. Maybe it won't. But it won't take today. Fuck you cancer; today is mine. And I'll take it, every day I get it.

Like That Idea

I created a spreadsheet for Mihailo with all the supplements and got the okay to take them. The pills I could add into my weekly pill container. But there were pills four times a day now, not two, so I hauled bottles back and forth to work and set pill taking times to get them all down. I made three to four shakes a day, in addition to my veggie shakes. I drank a separate concoction another four times a day made up of powdered fruits and veggies to increase my nutrient consumption. They weren't all that good, but they weren't gross either.

I took the pills and shakes and fish oil piously, every day; I did not miss a dose. I googled "Killer T cells attacking cancer" and found hundreds of videos posted from research facilities all over the globe. The imagery was absolutely fascinating. Blob-shaped killer cells with dozens of arms floating in suspension. When they find cancer, those arms probe into the cancer cell, disintegrating it. Every one of those videos had the equivalent of an Enya soundtrack in the background, sometimes a little more triumphant, but usually ethereal and dreamy, which fit the imagery. I watched these videos and then envisioned the process occurring in my body every night. I figured, can't hurt.

The plan was to revisit Dr. Peterson every six weeks and retest my body chemistry, reevaluate which supplements I'd need to continue to clean myself up. In the meantime, I'd continue my conventional treatments as well.

After about a month on the new supplements, it was time for an appointment with Mihailo. I didn't have a body scans at that appointment, but we did get my blood test results back. And guess what, there were notable differences. My white blood cells, primarily the neutrophils, the good guys, were up—a lot. They were in the normal range, even though the chemo pill I was on was a destroyer of neutrophils. For the last six months, we'd been adjusting the amount of chemo I was taking to maximize the dosage, without tanking my neutrophils to dangerously low levels that would put me at serious risk of infection. We watched my neutrophils a lot. I was steadily at a level that was still below normal but kept me one toe in the safe zone.

But after only one month on these supplements, my neutrophils more than doubled.

"Heather, my neutrophils were 2.3!" I exclaimed from the parking lot of the cancer center.

"Holy shit!" she said to match my excitement, and then, "What does that mean?"

"It means I'm now in the normal range."

"Whatever. You've never been normal."

I laughed, "Normal is like 1—7. I'm at 2.3! Heather 2.3! And it's data, my data." I was so excited I had to keep myself from flying. "Heather, maybe all these supplements are working."

I heard her start to cry softly, trying to hide it, "Maybe they are."

My neutrophils dropped back down the next month, but my cancer marker did as well. And it kept dropping. My scans kept showing reductions in cancer. We didn't know what was behind that—the alternative or conventional treatments. But as months went on, I started feeling like the diet and supplements were doing some of the lifting anyway. The idea of being on chemotherapy for the rest of your life is so discouraging; I wanted off the chemo med. But I wasn't sure I had the guts to drop the conventional treatments. I wasn't entirely confident in the alternative approach. But if it was possible that the supplements were working, maybe it was time to try. When I was about seven months into the supplements, I talked to Mihailo about making a change.

"So, could I stop taking these pills for a while, and then get back on them?" My own skepticism making me nervous to even ask. Mihailo was as open as an oncologist could be, but he was a conventionally trained oncologist. This was not in his bag of tricks.

He studied me, trying to figure out my angle. "You could. What are you thinking?"

I explained my concern that the two treatments were working against each other. On the integrative side, I was working to build my immune system, but on the conventional side, I was tearing it down with the lowering of my white blood cells. "Now might be the time to try things, to see if this integrative treatment can work, before I'm too far along and don't have any wiggle room at all, right?" Mihailo looked at me intently, remaining perfectly still. "I'm considering stopping the conventional treatments for a little while," I blurted out finally.

Mihailo continued to watch me and nodded slowly, before looking straight down at the floor. After a few seconds, he opened his mouth to say something, but then thought better of it and closed it again. Furrowed brow. Still staring at the floor. He paused for another few seconds, then took a deep breath again, but let it out without any words. When he went to wind up the third time and hesitated, I couldn't help but smile. Finally, he deflated and said softly, "I don't like that idea very well." He looked up to me and said, "Michele, I would worry for you."

And then, for the first time, I saw the tiniest chink in the armor. The first little bit outside of his even, measured presentation that was full concern and a little fear. In a cadence just a hair faster than normal, he said, "Michele, things are going so well. I just don't know why we'd give the cancer more estrogen." He raised his hands in a small shrug and looked around the room with torment before looking back to me.

"Well, it's not the hormonal med. It's more the chemo med that I'm worried about."

"Oh." he grimaced. "I think that's a good drug. You're tolerating it so well. I think that it really helps, I just..." he stopped himself then and closed his eyes for a second as if bracing himself. "Michele, I'll help you with whatever you want to do." He opened his eyes as if forcing himself to get behind those words as he said them again, "Whatever you want, I'll help."

I think there's some oath that doctors have to take. Something along the lines of putting your patients' needs and interests before your own. I could google it. I'd rather believe that I have a doctor who cares that much about me.

"It's the neutrophils I'm worried about." I tell him. "We've taken them down to just a hair above dangerous. The chemo just destroys them."

"The neutrophils do a lot for the immune system." Mihailo was getting excited now. He saw a compromise. "But there are other components of the white blood cells that do a lot, too. Like lymphocytes."

"Are my lymphocytes low too?"

"We didn't test for them as part of the routine labs."

"Can we?"

"Yes." Mihailo rolled his chair over to the computer to order up the test. He looked excited, like this might satisfy me, and we could both feel like we're doing everything we could to keep me alive. "We can run it from the draw you already had without taking another blood sample."

"Okay, so if the lymphocytes come back normal, then we could think of it like a good portion of my white blood cells aren't compromised. And I could stay on both treatments."

Mihailo was back to his even self. He was relieved, "Okay. If you're okay with that."

It was enough for me to keep it up with both kinds of treatments. Because the truth was that the 'what ifs' that ate away at my edges at night were hungrier on the alternative side. When it came down to it, I trusted the process behind the conventional science more. I shocked myself that I was even comfortable enough to consider something outside the box. I had to look for every option. That much I knew. I didn't want to look back and think, "I wish I would have…" I had to know that I was doing everything I could. Even if it was just the conversation, I needed to exhaust every option. If there was enough evidence that I'd have at least some white blood cells left, maybe I could keep going on both of them. For now.

Growing

The bottom line was that things were working. Which felt awesome. I sent out a message on my blog to let everyone know how well it was going and that we could pay attention to things besides cancer.

Posted by Michele, January 23, 2017

Hey everyone,

If you're from Wi or Pittsburgh, yesterday was a rough day for football. Maybe you'll need some good news to get over it. I'm happy to oblige.

My scan last week came back good! The lymph nodes in my chest shrunk, so everything in that area is nearly normal. Spots in the liver are still there. Most of them are still super tiny, hardly visible, shrinking. This is

GREAT news. It appears that treatments are working. Phew. AND! the scans confirm that I now have awesome abs. Yeah... I've been working out pretty regularly. We compared the scans and we could see the increased awesomeness of my six-pack abs.

The relief of a good scan makes it so easy to find humor. They're the easiest posts to write.

I had it nailed. Until I didn't. About eight months later, a CT scan had mixed results. Most of my cancer spots were gone, except one stubborn spot in my liver. Possibly a new spot, or maybe one of those tiny, little specks of gray in a previous image. Mihailo and I scrolled through the images, eyes squinted as we strained to see something a shade darker. *It could have been that one. Maybe. It's hard to tell. It might be a new one.* I felt my throat start to tighten. Either way it was a new blob that measured one centimeter in diameter. It was growing, quickly.

Mihailo said, "Since the rest of the spots are responding well to treatments, maybe this one grew and then was dying back since the last CT scan." If I didn't know him well by then, I wouldn't have picked up on his lack of conviction.

"But that's less likely."

He nodded, "The scan is inconclusive. A PET scan measures cellular activity so it would confirm if the cells are growing or dying."

I looked back to the CT scan images and reminded myself to take it one step at a time. To not get ahead of myself. To not start wondering what this meant. To just breathe. But it wasn't working. "So, a PET scan is the next step?" I said with my voice starting to shake.

"Yes. Then we'll know if a portion of the cancer has mutated and is resistant to the therapy." We didn't want resistance. Not yet. Resistance would move us on to the next drug in line. And my clock would start ticking a little faster. It would mean my alternative treatments weren't helping either. It would mean I was really stage IV, and it was looking like I wasn't going to be able to get out. Mihailo was talking about treatment options if cancer was growing, but I couldn't hear him. "We don't do PET scans here in Ashland. We should be able to get one scheduled in Duluth sometime next week."

"Okay, so we'll just get that scan and see what it says." I said and Mihailo nodded. "And maybe we'll be pleasantly surprised." He raised his eyebrows with possibility and nodded again. "But probably not." He conceded with a singular, slower nod. I was cracking. I needed to get out of there. My lips started to tremble as I said, "Okay."

"I'm sorry, Michele. Do you want me to call Jon?"

"No. I'm fine." I started to stand up. "So, can I just leave now?"

"Yeah. We'll call in a few days to set up the appointment." Mihailo stood up with me.

"Sounds good. Thanks." I stood up slowly to contain my fight or flight response. I kept my head down as I turned to walk out of the room. Mihailo followed me. He walked me out, past the other exams room and the front desk, in a slow and steady, panic-containing pace. Other nurses and staff moved around us, but I didn't dare look at any of them. We both looked straight ahead and said nothing, but I could feel his attention on me.

"I'm okay," I lied.

He said, "Okay," knowing I wasn't. Tears started falling when I walked out of the cancer center and into the lobby of the neighboring clinic. A clinic where people waited for much more mundane appointments. I wondered how many people walked out of the cancer center unable to stop a tear squeaking out, how many broke down as they walked through easy sickness land. I couldn't remember how many times I'd done it myself.

I was so certain that my time wasn't up on that med. I was sure of it. All the research indicated that it should have worked for at least another year. I thought I'd at least outperform the average. With all the integrative treatments I was adding on—I mean I was drinking spinach juice four times a day and taking 82 pills an hour—I thought it would at least get me a little further on down the road.

It was only a few months ago that I played a little game at an appointment called *Name Those Footsteps*! I'd listen to footsteps outside my examine room, and guess which ones were his. Nope, that's not Mihailo, too noisy. Nope, too much clacking on those steps. Wrong pace in that person; they're not stopping at this door. I sat in the exam room fully entranced by my game because I had nothing, *nothing* to worry about. When I was so assured that my treatments were working so well and no concern about cancer's eminent advance. Was it after my last appointment that I walked out of the cancer center and called my sister with light banter, another appointment crossed off with a sigh of uneventful relief? Not after this appointment.

"It's never going to end," I sobbed to her. "It's just going to keep going and going like this."

I waited while they cleared the test with insurance. I walked around hollow and numb while they arranged for the radioactive tracer to get shipped up to our hospital. But I didn't google a PET scan, what exactly it measured. What PET even stood for. I wasn't even curious.

I dealt by faking it. I kept moving. I paid attention to the girls and their light.

Post PET

"Hello, hello!" I called out as I walked up the back stairs into the house. Jon was at work. Lily was at Norwegian camp. (No, we're not Norwegian, but she was infatuated with this camp and Norwegian culture.)

Caitlin peeked out from the dining room and blurted out, "Are you radioactive?" I hadn't told her about my scan today, but I guess Jon did.

"Yeah, I had the scan." I took a step towards the kitchen, and she took a couple panicked steps backwards.

"So. you're, like, emitting something?"

"I'll just keep a little more to myself for a day. It breaks down really quickly." She wasn't buying this for a second. It was too weird and foreign. "It's okay, Caitlin. It won't travel that far."

"How far does it go?"

"It's mostly really little kids that they're worried about. I should stay three feet or so away from them. You're fine."

"Is this three feet?" She looked terrorized at the distance between us.

"No, you're about ten feet away from me right now." I smiled at her and heard the guys who were working on a remodel of our upstairs bathroom. Proximity made it impossible for them to not hear us. And equally impossible for them hearing us not to feel misplaced. Awkward! Cancer is so awkward!

"Is that going to take years off your life?"

"No honey. It's not like that."

"Is it going to take years off my life?"

"No. Not at all."

"Days?"

"No. Not even days."

"What is it?"

"It's really interesting actually," I said as I put away my lunch containers, to try to make it feel like a normal day. "They gave me a radioactive sugar. And then they look for cells eating the sugar."

"Because cancer eats sugar."

"Yep, kind of like that." I put my purse on the counter and Caitlin backed further into the dining room.

"How long will you, have it?"

"It breaks down really quickly. It'll be gone by tomorrow."

"Can you sleep with Dad?"

"Oh yeah. They said that would be fine." I figured I'd leave out their instructions to not have sex and not touch him.

"Do you think he'll even want to sleep with you?"

Probably not. "It's really fine, honey. It's not a problem. Want to have burritos for dinner?"

"Um..." she stopped making eye contact. "No, I'm not really hungry." Caitlin was always hungry.

"Are you sure?"

"How about Dad cooks tonight."

I see. "Okay. That sounds good. Hey, did you find that cake recipe?"

"I did! I found one with strawberries and chocolate. It looks *so* good. Come here, Mom I'll show you." She kept looking over her shoulder as she walked toward the computer, so I let her stay a few steps ahead of me. The guys from upstairs snuck out the front door while she showed me an obscene tower of chocolate. The distraction took but was short lived.

"Why did you have that scan now, Mom?"

"They just check up on me every once and while." I couldn't tell her. I lied to myself that I was waiting until the results came in to spare her the worry. But really it was that I was just barely hanging on. I needed a distraction. I needed chocolate strawberry cake.

"With the radioactive stuff? Isn't that bad for you?"

"I won't get those scans often. Just every once and while."

We revisited the conversation of my radiance every few minutes. Caitlin simultaneously unable to leave me alone and unable to stop asking about my radiation. But the cakes eventually won out. When Jon got home an hour later, we were still looking at frosted towers with obscene decoration.

"Hey mister," I said as he came in. He smiled at me and then we both looked at the computer pretending to be interested in cakes. From Caitlin, I wanted distraction, but from Jon, I wanted him to pry me for every detail. I wanted him to be unable to take his eyes off me. I wanted him to share my fear so much that he couldn't stop himself from wrapping me up in him, radiating or not. I wanted to tell him the size of the gear needed to close that metal door, so thick it moved slower than molasses, and that I sat alone for an hour in a lead lined vault to protect the staff from the toxic whatever they just injected me with. And we would talk about how unbelievable it is that this is actually freaking happening to me. But instead we both stared at the computer screen and acted like we were interested in cakes.

After ten minutes, Jon said, "Come on. Let's go kayaking. Water makes everything better."

We headed out to the garage to ready the boats. Jon set them up on the trailer. For years, I listened with annoyance as I was corrected in the appropriate strap placement, tightness, and tag end securing of securing the boats. You see, there is only one correct and very specific way to secure the straps to kayaks on a trailer. Jon's way. I did not willingly succumb to the role of unsuccessful student in strap tying, adjusting my technique only to have Jon take it apart and redo it every time. Because that's hella annoying. But now, I think of the guy who made me a fluid sack satchel and instead I grabbed the paddles, skirts, and water bottles.

We headed a few blocks down to an old coal dock that was a wide and rough gravel drive extending a few hundred yards into the lake. The loading cargo days had long past for this dock, but fisherman made good use of it. Teens jumped off it occasionally.

A few years ago, Jon rushed home with the excitement and energy of a howling storm at the dock. A steady, raging wind was blowing in so strong from the south he had to lean into it to stay upright. Charged by the storm, he rallied us to bundle up in rain gear and get out there to see if we could fly with a giant blue tarp as a sail. Six to eight-foot waves slammed into the dock, drenching us in wave spray from 30 feet away. Lily's friend, Sam, was with us, which made for one person to hold each corner of the tarp and one to scream over the wind with directions. *Hold your end down low! What? Down low! Dad's taller! He should take a top corner!* We were a circus of massive blue tarp and running in circles, with the gusts making us stumble and clumsy. *It slipped out of my hand! Don't let it go! Okay! I got it!* And when we'd position it just right, the force of the relentless gales would fill the tarp, wind that could carry us into flight. Soaking wet and trying to hold position, we'd laugh at possibility. *I feel it! That's it! It's pulling me!* We spent nearly an hour chasing that tarp in the storm, carefree with laughter and adventure. I think we might have flown, just a little bit.

I looked down the dock and wondered if I'd ever feel that again.

We pulled over to a shaded beach at the base of the coal dock. An easy entry point for kayaking. It had reached the mid 80's that day, with hardly a breeze, which for us is an ungodly heat wave. We were all ready for the cold waters of Lake Superior

"I can't believe this is the first time we've had our boats out this year," I said to Jon.

"It's kind of embarrassing," said Jon as he opened the tailgate of the truck. "We need to at least get the dust off them." Opie walked slowly to the edge of the truck bed. He leaned against Jon to be carried out of the truck, fully aware that he was no longer a jumper. Jon smiled and set him gently on the ground.

I picked up Ava, our new puppy and let her down to join Opie in running around the trucks. It didn't take much to talk Jon into getting another dog. He'd been adamant for years prior that there would be no more dogs after Opie. Lil worked on him for days to get a new pup, looking for every angle to change his mind. I let it play out for a while, trying not to smile—no one likes a gloater.

Finally, I turned to Lil and said, "I got this honey." I looked back to Jon and said simply, "I think getting a puppy would make me happy."

With that, Jon let his head fall forward in resignation. A co-worker knew of a litter of lab/ bernese mountain dog mixes, and we brought one home a few weeks later. We all fell in love with her instantly, and none of us more than Jon. She was a bright spot of light that summer, filling us with joy as a distraction from the fear. We all held her a little more softly in thanks for that.

Ava and Opie rambled around the beach as we untied the kayaks and grabbed our PFDs. Jon has trained us all that they are personal floatation devices. Not life jackets. Caitlin helped me carry my boat to the water.

"Want some help getting your boat?" I asked her.

She turned back to the truck and said, "I'll get it myself." As I got my boat ready, I heard her straining up by the trailer.

"You have to hold your boat higher," Jon was telling her. She had the cockpit of her boat resting on her PFD on her shoulder, but she was struggling with the weight of the boat and kept trying to heave it up.

"It is up there, but it keeps hitting my hips." She shifted it again.

"If you're carrying it right it won't do that. Not to the side like that, more forward."

"I am doing that. My hips are in the way." Caitlin was long legged and short waisted. With a boat so wide in the middle, the geometry didn't work in her favor.

"It shouldn't be," Jon insisted. Unwilling to accept that body shapes are different.

"It is," Caitlin insisted. Unwilling to accept that body shapes are the same.

"Want me to show you?" He was dying to show her.

"No."

"Want some help?" I asked her.

"No, I've got it," she said as she struggled the last few steps. That's my girl.

We launched from the beach. Paddled along the sandstone cliffs, I looked around and saw no other boats in sight. The lake was ours. I felt the rhythm of my boat gliding along the surface and the drip of water sliding down my paddle. In only a handful of strokes, beach transitioned to rocky cliffs. The shoreline we paddled was regularly hammered with six to seven-foot waves that pried boulders as big as VW bugs from the cliffs, scattering them in the water and on the shoreline. Birch trees and aspens lined the cliffs, with dogwoods in between them. I saw tansy with their bright, yellow flowers, perfectly round hanging from the cliff. Later, daisies took their spot, reaching to show off their delicate white flowers to the sky. With each stroke of quiet and motion, color and rhythm, I felt myself become a part of the lake.

This. This was what I needed. With every stoke, I more immersed in the present. The present was a much better place to be.

I looked back to Jon and Caitlin paddling further from the shore. Jon had a sit on top fishing kayak, a massive, heavy hog of a boat with an open deck just big enough for Ava in the front and Opie in the back. Caitlin followed him, giddy for the dog's attention, and for Jon's. I thought of the girls as eager little munchkins, how they revered his adventure and paddling prowess. I saw his sincere reveling of being "that guy." I glanced further behind us and watched the masts of sailboats at the marina turned to matchsticks. We were headed away from development and towards the more undeveloped peace of the lake. I just wanted the lake.

I leaned to the right to head a little closer to them.

"Look at Ava, Mom!" hollered Caitlin when she saw me. Ava was standing on the very edge of the kayak, frantic and distracted by everything around her. She bit at the water and slid a bit closer to the edge of the boat; she nearly leapt up to chomp at a passing fly; she flipped her head towards the ducks skimming the surface on the other side of the boat. Ava was totally in the present. And her lightness was contagious.

"Think she's going for a swim tonight?" I asked.

"She might." Jon couldn't take his eyes off her. He was smitten with that dog, a catchy love that radiated from him, I couldn't help but catch some of it. We paddled around a small, stubborn island, with a few scrappy pines still clinging to it, despite the wind's attempts to tear them from it. They were worn from the effort, thin in the top, but miraculously managed to stay rooted securely to it. I admired their resolve.

"Hey Caitie Ray," I gestured to the open water. "If you were going to paint that, what colors would you use?" She considered the water. "Water is usually painted as blue, right? But there's hardly any blue in there. I see purple on the back of each ripple, lines and lines of them as far as you can see. And yellow and whites."

"I might use some blue." she studied the water. "Mixed in with the purple."

"Yeah, I see that. And the sky is such a gentle shade of pastels."

"Pastels? You'd use pastels?" She wasn't impressed with my pastel choice. "But then look to the shore, Mom. It's totally different." The sandstone cliffs, now thirty feet high, shaded the water turned it to dark, rich tones. We were buffered from the slight wind by the point up ahead, leaving the water still as glass, with just the slightest of swirling color. "I'd use greens, black and brown. No blue in there at all."

"It's amazing how different it is from one side of the boat to the other," I agreed.

"I'd use all the colors," Jon said playfully as he paddled around us. I grinned, watching him move his boat around with a subtle adjustment of his paddle. Water was a part of him always.

"You make this weird expression sometimes, Mom," said Caitlin.

"How do you mean?"

"It's a look. It's, funny." She studied me.

"How?"

"I don't know."

"When do I do this?" I raised my eyebrows and look sideways at her.

"No, it's not that," she observed me sternly. This was her thing lately. She would tell me how I am like she was getting to know me for the first time. This was another of Caitlin's gifts. She takes the time to really see someone, to know who they are. *Mom, you're like, a really happy person. You love to laugh. You and Gammy and Heather all love to laugh. But you're quieter than they are. You're really nice, Mom too. You love everybody.* I was thankful and flattered that her observations were so far mostly positive. She had a sense already, even at fourteen, to keep the not so flattering observations to herself. A testament to her character. Or maybe she was waiting for sixteen for that. This look I had, she hadn't quite figured out, "It's kind of random."

Laughing, I asked her, "Well, what the heck is it?"

Until she was laughing too, "I don't know it's, weird."

"Is it flirty?"

"No. I mean, not really."

"You're making me sound sassy and spunky. I like that. Is it this?" I made my best *Oh yeah home slice, I'm all over it* kind of face.

"Yeah, um, don't do that Mom," and she paddled ahead in embarrassment.

We rounded a point to a less sheltered part of lake. Peaceful, lazy waves about six inches high lulled us further into the cadence of the lake. The sandstone cliffs were stunning, broad strokes of deep orange and warm browns. The layers of rock were like a petrified stack of pancakes topped with tall pines, spruce with rich, and varied greens of shrubs billowing over the cliff.

"There's the cave," Jon pointed towards it with his paddle.

The squat cave was framed by a ten-foot vertical buttress of sandstone. I let the waves gently carry me to her. As I coasted into the dark, damp cave, ducking down to fit with just a foot or two above my head, I felt the temperature drop by at least ten degrees. I was encased in a world thirty feet in diameter that filtered the sounds of the wind, birds and water, leaving only deep, baritone gongs as water caressed the inner hollows of the cave. Each grumble varied in pitch depending on which small cavern hosted the wave. I was in the belly of a peaceful giant, moaning in her sleep. I closed my eyes and felt the gentle rise and fall of the water, felt the rich sound of water.

I opened my eyes to take in the cave. The sandstone was darker here, more streaks of dark green, more variations in deep red. I paddled myself around and saw shrubs rustling at the top of the entrance. Then, I saw Jon and Caitlin far from the cave, beyond the shadow of the cliff and bathed in light. They were holding their paddles high above their heads, rocking their hips side to side to get their boats up on edge. Jon was training her to feel the boat's limits. She shrieked when water entered her cockpit. She took it just a little too far, but that was the point, to learn the bounds. I saw their laughter and banter but couldn't hear what they were saying. It made me feel way too far away, too separate, so I hurried out of the cave to join them.

When I approached, they started splashing each other. Jon was telling Caitlin to take it easy, but moderation was not in her nature, nor his. Caitlin slapped her blade at Jon and then started frantically paddling away. An excuse to show off his paddling power, Jon dug in and set off after her. This was not my game, so I followed steadily behind them, easily able to keep up because my boat was so much faster. He caught up and sent a light spray at her. It was her turn now, and she set up to get him again. She was poised to douse him. Jon looked calmly back at her, displaying the confidence that whatever she'd throw at him, he'd return three-fold. She tested it, a small splash towards the edge of his boat.

I said, "You might want to think about that, Caitlin."

"Come on, Dad. You should be a good role model. Be kind and forgiving."

"I'll forgive you after I splash you."

"That's not being a good role model."

"It is," he countered. "I'm teaching you to never give in." He said it like he was kidding. We all knew he wasn't. Jon doesn't roll over for anything or anyone. Caitlin has inherited this trait.

I shook my head with a smile, "The battle of wills between you two."

"I'm not being willful. She is."

"No, he is." And with that Jon sent a full paddle full of water all over the front of her. She was briefly stunned by the cold water, a face full of it. Jon giggled and paddled on; Caitlin tearing off after him. They spent the rest of the evening laughing and splashing and chasing each other back to shore. God, how I loved them.

The paddle relaxed me, helped me let go of the inner war of my thoughts. By the time we settled into bed, I could let it go. I started to read as Jon got in bed beside me.

"Do you want to talk about today?" he asked.

I didn't.

"What did Mihailo say about the scan?" I turned to look at him. He was lying on his side looking at me, his eyebrows raised in concern. He really wanted to know.

I put my book down, annoyed that after he finally got me not thinking about the scan, he now wanted me to relive it. "The spot in the liver was bright."

"Bright is bad?"

"Yeah," I was looking at the ceiling but started seeing those images again. "They're worried about the spot in my liver and another in my spine."

"But nothing came up in your back on any of other scans?"

"I guess CT scans don't pick up bone mets as well. But the PET gives a different view," The despair that the lake had washed away started to creep back.

"Can they treat it?"

"Yep. There's a new type of radiation. Very targeted for small spots. They could probably treat both spots at the same time. I'll need an MRI to get set up to treat the liver spot, so that will confirm if my spine has cancer too. They're hoping to set that up in a few days." I looked over to Jon and saw that his eyes were nearly closed. "Are you *sleeping*?" I shouted. It startled him awake.

"No, no." He barely opened his eyes before closing them again.

"You've got to be kidding me."

He reached out for me and said, "I'm awake. An MRI...." And his eyes opened briefly again.

I threw his hand off me. "I'm radiating, remember? Forget it." I rolled over and turned out the light. Un-freaking-believable. He was asleep before I settled on to my side with my back to him. *Either take my mind off it or don't,* I thought. *But don't suck me back into this nightmare and then fall asleep.* I thought about sleeping downstairs.

It must be exhausting to be the caregiver. Jon's job was exceptionally demanding at this time of year. It always was. He could clone himself and still not be able to satisfy all the demands on him. I was sure he rushed home that day leaving a pile of unfinished business. He wouldn't show a hint of that. He didn't give me the desperate attention I wanted from him when he got home, but he did give me what I needed, and what Caitlin needed, with the trip to the lake. He was trying to anticipate my emotional needs constantly, as they swung from one extreme to the other. *Starve for my every thought! Don't ask me about anything*! And it was like that. All the time.

I wondered if he had someone to talk to about this mess. If you're the guy who says, 'Ugh, it is just so *exhausting* to try to anticipate what she needs again and *again*," you're an asshole. We morally assume that partners will be there in time of need. *Till death do us part.* It's easier to believe of yourself and your partner when the thick grime of serious illness is somewhere far off in the distance. In practice, the stress of cancer's chaos was monumentally consuming. For the caregiver, it must feel isolating and consistently draining to be sucked into the illness of someone you love, knowing that you can't understand how it feels for them. I decided to just let him sleep.

Dirt Lip and Diesel Bear

I waited for radiology to schedule my MRI. Time continued to pass. Once it was scheduled, I had to wait for the test. Waited again for my appointment to see the results. I had to distract myself from all this waiting. Jon and Caitlin were gone for the day to pick up Lily from Norwegian camp. (Again, not Norwegian! But whatever!) I almost let cancering talk me into spending the day sitting on the couch with the shades drawn, sulking. But it was a beautiful day. Blue skies without a cloud, perfect temperature and the slightest breeze. The day felt alive. It was enough to shove me over the hump of resistance and go do something.

Be outside.

Throughout years of cancering, I'd developed a suite of tactics, mantras, that help me get by. I headed to the mountain bike trails just fifteen minutes from home. The parking lot was empty. Perfect. I was here to make myself well and needed some solo time to do that. The trails here were put in only a few years ago. As it goes in northern Wisconsin, people just up and make things happen. *Hey, I've got an idea, let's do this.* And off they go to build new mountain bike trails: build a coalition, form a vision, raise funds, and host work parties. I used to think these things just happened. I didn't think about the passionate people who overcame the mess and bureaucratic hurdles and logistics to make the fun stuff come to life for the rest of us. That day I really felt it, the work of others that helped me get up off the couch.

Practice gratitude.

It was my first ride of the season. I hopped on my bike and left the openness of the parking lot for the woods on a narrow track of compacted sand. Sunlight filtered through the canopy of mixed hardwoods towering 50 feet overhead. The first mile of trail was a steady uphill, slowing me down and also letting me soak up the riot of ferns and soft plants on the forest floor in endless varieties of shapes and greens. Under all that new growth, last year's dead, matted leaves were readily giving up their place. But I couldn't focus on all those intricacies. The trail was constantly changing, cutting across the slope in sharp switchbacks, narrowing then opening up again through a maze of small rocks. I tensed up as I passed between two trees just wide enough for my handlebars. I spun around a sharply banked corner and shifted down even further to get up the hill. My heart rate was rising. I stood up to climb a steeper section of trail and felt the push-pull of my legs and arms. The feeling of work. The feeling of getting stronger.

Be active.

I finished the steady uphill and followed the trail through a gentle meander on flat ground. Now I could pick up speed. Trees were flying by me, the trail demanding my attention. Only when I was rounding a bend or cresting a hill could I get a quick glimpse at what was coming up next. I was getting my groove on, steering by tilting my bike from side to side. Around the next corner, I hit a section of rocks that bumped me right out of my confidence. I braced myself and slowed down, which only made the jostling worse. I strained to keep peddling. I tensed as each rock threw me to the side, and I overcorrected to get back to the trail. I was just about to get off my bike when I made it through the bumpy stretch.

Just keep moving forward through the rough parts.

Around the next bend, I reached the side of the hill dominated with conifers in dark, rich greens, shade that cooled the slope by a few degrees. The trail cut alongside a steep hill, the upslope only a hands-reach to my right and the ground dropping off sharply to my left. The trail's descent was interrupted by a series of dips through small drainages. The constant flow of up and down on such a fun ride left no room for cancering. A sharp turn revealed a fifteen-foot-long bridge about two-feet-wide. It was only a few feet off the ground, but consequences made me wish the bridge was just a little bit wider. I focused my attention on the far end of the bridge and peddled right across. When I first started riding, I would stare at the bridge as I crossed it, focused on the obstacles, the places I wanted to avoid. It made me steer myself right towards them. I learned that a simple shift in attention changed my direction to an easier course.

Focus on where you want to go, not on the obstacles in your way.

I crossed the bridge and stopped at the next trail junction to catch my breath and study the trail map. After the constant motion of biking, it was nice to be still, to feel the calm of the forest. I heard the rustle of a sneaky little critter rustling in the leaves behind me. I searched the ground to get a glimpse of it, but only heard its occasional scamper through the leaves. And then it stayed put, likely tired of my scrutiny. Smart critter. I turned back to the map to pick my route. I was at the junction of two trails - Dirt Lip and Diesel Bear. They looped in opposite directions and were about equal distance. I headed off to Dirt Lip on the right.

Dirt Lip was a similar mix of up and down, pulling me in deeper as I wound through the woods. With each turn, I was better able to anticipate and found myself riding with less hesitancy. I slowed at a fork in the trail just in time to see a sign with a green circle for the easier track and another sign with a black square pointing towards the more challenging features to the left. My life had enough challenge. I was after adrenaline without fear. I headed straight for the green.

Ahead I saw a tightly spaced series of humps, each about two feet tall. I wasn't yet over the first one when the next one came. Two, three, four humps. The trail was still headed downward, and I was picking up speed. Five. Six. The next bump was a little bigger. It pulled my front end sharply downward, threatening to launch me over my handlebars. On instinct, I shifted my weight far behind my seat for balance. I anchored in with my legs and reached far forward to let my arms follow the flow of my bike over the last three humps more steadily.

Know your anchor and get there.

The trail suddenly opened up from dense forest to a patch of shrubs. I slowed down to get my bearings. This isn't where I thought I would end up. I was back at that first junction, which put me only a mile to my car. I needed a little more. I turned around and headed back through the same meandering stretch of woods. When I reached the rocky stretch this time, I was ready for it. I downshifted before I got there and stood up in my seat to power through. My bike still rattled across the rocks, but I could roll with it more easily. I focused on the trail ahead, and let my legs and arms be the shocks. I was still bumped around, but much steadier this time.

The same path can be made easier by the way you ride it.

I knew what I needed to do to get through this day, this moment. Sometimes it's just really, really hard to do it. Made harder by having to do it over and over again. It was a nag, cancer was. An obnoxious annoying nag. As the years of cancering piled on, the weight of it made me simply not want to do it anymore. Knowing I'm stuck with it just made it a heavier load to carry.

Each scan brought nervous anticipation with a different flavor of anxiety disguised as hope. At first, I hoped there wouldn't be any growth. I rode a wave of confidence for a while that all my medications and diet adjustments and supplements would work. And cancer would retreat. But the first bad scan knocked me back a notch. I lowered my expectations. I continued to hope for more time than average, even if shy of a full recovery. *Please let it just be that one spot.* And now yet another scan and its results to await. *Please let it just be in my liver. Please not in my spine as well.* I didn't have any more energy for the mania that is riding cancer. The hope-defeat cycle, so extreme at both ends, was too much to bear.

My MRI was in three days. Three days to wait, three days to think. I left the bike trails a little less obsessed with wondering if my spine was clear. I let it be a subtle wish, let it speak its peace, and then I asked it to go sit elsewhere. I replaced the anxieties over the scan with my mantras from the bike ride, my ways to make it through the moment.

Cancer was an unwilling hitchhiker, a burrowing thistle of a hitchhiker. But it was still my ride. Whatever this week's MRI results would be, I'd ride it out.

How to Get By

I sat on my couch to write out a new blog post. It had been a while, and I struggled with what to say. When my cancer returned, I kept my resilient cancer-fighting persona for the first few posts. Same recipe, same intentions. But my disease was changing, and I with it. The intensity of cancering was increasing; it was getting a whole lot grittier.

People are curious. They think they want to know. But most of the time they really don't. Too many bodily fluids. Too many procedures that shock and repulse. Grandstanding this cancer in my posts with details that made people grimace then fall silent, save pity, was no help to any of us. With shorter intervals of steady pseudo-normalcy, stage IV cancering was getting too messy for a crowd.

I re-read the last post I wrote. It was from nearly a year earlier after a good scan on my first medication. I could feel the joy and hope in every word of it. The posts with good news were always the easiest ones to write.

In the months that followed, I was stable. There was nothing to report.

I almost sent an update when that one spot started to grow; that was a change. But it now felt absurd to be as open as I was during the first rodeo. The intensity of cancer consuming your liver, leading to the end of you, is about as intimate as it gets. My mass email list came from my first rodeo - the nice friendly cancer that I'd just have to endure a few treatments for, and then I'd be fine. Some on that list were my inner circle; the ones I wanted, needed to go there with. Others I wasn't as close with. I didn't know how to write a post that would fit for all.

I tried.

Posted by Michele, May 22, 2018

Hi everyone,

It's been a while since I wrote to you all. It's been an active past few months. The last time I wrote, I was on a med that really seemed to be doing the trick. We were all glad to see that. But then, it stopped working so well. At first it looked like there was just one spot of cancer in my liver that was resistant, so we radiated it. A scan a few months later determined that it wasn't just that one spot; cancer was growing in other liver spots too. But good news! It's not in my spine. Had a scare about that, but a follow up scan that came back clear. With the progression in the liver, we had to put the first medication to bed. Knowing that there are a finite number of these meds to go through makes it tough to finish one up. Especially since the average amount of time

*on that medication is 22 months. I only made it 12 until
my cancer showed resistance. Bummer.*

*So, I tried another med. But that one tried to kill me before
the cancer did. Ugh. Lots of throwing up, no anti-nausea
med that helped. The med didn't seem to work on holding
back my cancer anyway, so we had to dump that one as
well. The one I'm on now is only slightly less mean. And it's
added a complete aversion to food to my list of side effects.
It's like every meal is a writhing plate of maggots. I dropped
50 pounds in four months. Not a good time. Overall, I've
gone from a size 14 to a baggy sized 6. So, I had to stop
my cancer fighting diet because we're all worried about me
starving to death now...*

I stopped. Does anyone really want to know things? That post
was simply the complaints of my reality. I imagined hundreds of
messages landing in inboxes all throughout my town and then
seeing my neighbors, my coworkers over the next few days.

"Hi, how's it going?" I'd ask them.

"Oh. Hi," they'd respond, avoiding eye contact. "Yeah... I -
ah - I got your post."

"Oh, yeah."

"Yeah, um..." Begins thinking about terminal illness and has
no idea what to say.

"It's okay."

"I'm so sorry, Michele." It would end there. Where else could
it go? Ugh. No, thank you.

I deleted the message. In past years, we all enjoyed the triumphant banter on my website. It no longer served, wasn't part
of this ride. I didn't want to invite in a few hundred acquain-

tances to watch me flail in uncertainty while my body fell apart at the seams.

I thought about what I wanted out of the site. The purpose of this website was to help me. I tried again, with less detail.

Posted by Michele, May 22, 2018

Hi everyone,

It's been a long time since I've sent around one of these updates. It's been hard to know whether or not to send one. Stage IV cancering is very active. And very uncertain. And... well... it's full of a lot of really not fun things. It's amazing what you can get used to though.

I will spare you the details, and just say that for right now, I'm roughly stable. I realize this is possibly the lamest update ever, but... well...that's all I got. Would it have been better to just send nothing? Hard to say.

I read it over a few times. It was cryptic and almost ominous in its lack of information. Like the thing behind it was worse than I was letting on. Because it was. My alternative medicines were failing me; my conventional meds were working 50 percent shy of average. Did I want to talk about this with everyone I knew? I wondered again what the purpose was. I couldn't think of an answer but hit send anyway.

I started another email list. This one with my closest friends and family who make up a more deeply entwined source of comfort in my inner circle of support. These were the people I could call crying, that I had called crying, and then could laugh with.

The beautiful, loving people who would take my calls any time of day, never knowing which version of me would be on the other end. The ones who know when a text simply means hello, and when "hello" is a cry for help.

During her own cancer treatments, Margaret Feinberg called this group the Fellowship of the Afflicted. Those people who "know the great unspeakables of pain and loss," and have a more innate sense of what someone suffering needs as a result. Those in the fellowship seem to get this. My inner circle housed the ones who had been closest to me for years. A few unexpected friends joined in, just showing up again and again. There were others who dropped off; the calls, texts, and visits just disappeared. It's a hard, heavy thing cancer. I had no energy to get through the hurt of rejection at my greatest time of need. I let them go.

My message to my inner circle was more real. More open. Not hiding the shitty parts.

Email by Michele Wheeler, May 23, 2018

> *This stage IV cancering is kind of a disaster. I'll just come out and say that the last five months have really sucked. The chemo portion of the treatments have been so incredibly hard on me. We're trying to get a handle on the nausea and diarrhea but haven't had much luck yet. Nearly every med I'm on causes fatigue, so that I'm upright at all is a miracle. Feeling so sick makes the emotional part of this a lot harder.*

When I wrote that last line, I realized that it was the first time I admitted how badly I was hurting. I was so focused on the fight, on getting out of that windowless doorless room, that I didn't stop to even acknowledge that I might not make it out. It was a step towards acceptance that I had not allowed before.

> *I found another lump in my neck. Small as a tic tac. But it grew to the size of a marble in about two weeks. Looks like I have a very aggressive cancer. I'm so freaking sick of feeling sick on this med, sick of burning through yet another med in only half the time of most. It's horrifying.*

> *I'm having a hard time. This is a hard time, the whole bit of it. This is not the cheerful cancer post. Cuz I'm not feeling very cheerful. There it is.*

> *Love yas,*
> *M*

I read it again. I saw in it that denial was wearing me thin just as much as the hope-defeat cycle. I was pissed off and exhausted, and I decided to stop pretending I wasn't. I hit send.

I thought it would be a release. A cathartic honesty that would let me set down the weight of façade I'd been holding for so long. But it didn't make me feel any better. It made me feel more pissed off and more exhausted and more bitter towards all those healthy assholes and their promised futures.

Cancer is impossible.

That's all it took. Just one glance towards my reality, and the grief I'd been bottling shattered into a flood. No warning, no wind up, no conscious thought that set off me off. One step, I'd be walking into one of the girls' volleyball tournaments. The next step, I'd get thrown straight into the suffocating spin of a hungry whirlpool. I was gone, reaching for safety in any direction until I'd find Jon and bury my face in his chest. We'd stand still, a rock in the stream of the mob of other parents giving wide birth to the hysterical woman and the man holding her with concern and confusion. After five to ten minutes, I was back on dry land, able to breathe and dry my eyes. I was determined not let my girls see me like that. Instead, I turned off all emotion and stayed hollow for the rest of the day, unable to feel and unable to explain why. I didn't know I'd just had a panic attack.

For a while I could control them. But that didn't last long. I started having them at work. I was cleaning my teacup, and in response to nothing, I started to sob silently. A co-worker came in talking quickly in the middle of a story. I could tell it was a light, funny story from the way her laughter snuck into every sentence. I stared at the sink, scrubbing that mug, but I couldn't even hear her. I put the mug down, stammering, "I can't. I mean. Sorry. But I..." She kept telling me it was okay as I backed out of the room making random sounds, because I didn't know how to explain.

Soon, the sadness shifted to rage. Autumn was at my place one night; the rest of my family was somewhere else. I was talking through my grief. About the things I'd miss. How it wasn't fair. How I didn't deserve this. Until I was completely consumed by fire. Talking turned to screams of fury. Screams that erupted from the whole of me again and again. I roared harder to push that rage out, wishing I'd explode, or that my guts would come out. Anything for release. I could not see or hear anything. I was gone from this world, reached around for some sort of anchor but ended up kneeling on the floor making guttural sounds of rage in between a steady stream of "FUCK!" and "NOOOOOO! NO! NO! NO!"

I looked around in panic, like I had to flee, but there was no safe ground anywhere. I wiped the tears and snot off my face and bawled so hard I couldn't stand. I pounded on the floor and screamed until my throat hurt, and I did not stop.

Autumn had been waiting me out in complete calm. She sat still on a stool on the other side of the kitchen. She didn't try to stop me. She didn't move. She never said a word. When I started losing the energy to scream, she asked, "Do you want to be touched?"

I shook my head no and then resumed shrieking until I wore myself out. After my screams subsided to whimpers, Autumn came over and sat next to me on the floor. I let myself fall into her to be held and cried more softly. After a few minutes, I asked, "Is this position horribly uncomfortable for you?"

"Eh, doesn't matter," she said. And then a few minutes later, "Well, maybe a little." Laughter through tears is the best feeling in the world. That and having a friend who isn't scared off by a panic attack gone to fury. Someone who will share your grief while making dinner, allowing a moment of normalcy if there's room for it, but not pushing away the pain when it comes back to dominate. Autumn's greatest gift to me is that she continues to see me, that person still in there, despite all the cancering and the pain that comes with it.

Jon got a smaller episode a few weeks later. He had no experience with this uninhibited explosion of pain. He stood helplessly beside me. He knew me as the one who got quieter when I got upset. The more that cold water poured over me in the canoe, the quieter I got. Not now. He stood beside me, feeling ill-equipped, frozen. But he stayed until the fury lost its steam, and I fell into him in sorrow. "I've never seen anything like that," he told me later, eyes wide. Neither had I, as spectator or performer.

They kept coming. I felt one start to brew at work and called Autumn desperately, "I need a place to go. Where should I go?"

"Meet me at the parking lot by power plant at the lake. I'll be there in five."

I drove down to the lake and sat in my car to avoid the cold and wind. I focused on steady, even breathing while I waited, reminding myself that Autumn would be there any second to keep me out of the whirlpool. I took stock of every real, tangible thing around me. I watched the waves roll in. Listened to calls of the gulls as they bickered over food scraps. Watched steam float gently out of the stacks at the top of the powerplant.

Autumn pulled up next to me then and hurried into my passenger seat. She talked, looking over at me every once and a while to see if I had anything to add. I stared at her in the lost emptiness on the edge of panic that had now become familiar as she keep talking. At some point, I found my voice and said, "I don't know what to do. I don't want to be this person, but I don't know how to stop it."

"Do you want to see someone at behavioral health?" she asked.

I considered it but was skeptical. When I told Mihailo what a hard time I was having, he suggested anti-depressants. But I didn't think I was depressed. I didn't have some chemical imbalance in my brain. I was just dealing with some really hard shit. I tried talking to the counselor at my cancer center in Ashland. I was actually feeling pretty calm that day, so I was able to spread out my reality for her objectively. When I was done, she looked visibly upset.

"Do you think this is something you can handle?" I asked her. Maybe it was because we were close in age; it was too close to home. Maybe it was because she was new to her career and had little experience working with the terminally ill. I respected that she couldn't help but feel the sadness in my reality and found a few more names to try out.

I went to Duluth to see if they had more experienced options. On the card of the next counselor, it said, "Helps patients with emotional challenges of cancer." When I reached her office, she hurried me in with frantic energy and before asking one single question, she started handing me brochures in rapid-fire about potential services I could tap into, starting with hospice. I sat speechless. I was not ready to talk about hospice yet. "Oh wait." She searched the ceiling to remember which patient she was talking to. "You don't live in Duluth, so that probably won't help." She chucked the brochure over her shoulder.

She paused just enough for me to get a word in, so I asked, "This brochure says that you provide emotional support to patients. Is that something you do?"

"Oh no, I'm not licensed in 'blah-blah-blah' therapy or this other kind of therapy. I've been thinking about going back to school to get a degree, but then a friend asked me, 'Do you really want to listen to people's sob stories all day?' I told her, 'Well, I pretty much do already, so I might as well get certified. Oh! Did I show this brochure about a group that helps families take their final trip together? Most go to Disney."

That woman should not be a therapist.

I stood up and left.

Back at the lake, I asked Autumn, "Is there anyone around here that can actually help me?" I was convinced there wasn't, convinced I was an abandoned woman on an island, left to figure this out on my own.

"I have someone in mind," Autumn said.

I made an appointment with Autumn's recommendation, Dave, the next week. He previously worked in close cooperation with an out-of-state cancer center. Dave hardly said a word during our first appointment. He listened with attendance that assigned no pressure. He welcomed every word and let me speak my sorrow uninterrupted.

I felt heard. He said I was carrying around a glass of pain so full to the brim, I had no space for one more shred of burden. A glass so full of hurt, it separated me from myself, from those I love. He prescribed mostly anti-anxiety medication to create some extra room in that glass. He reminded me that these medications wouldn't take the glass from me, wouldn't empty it completely, but they could stop the relentless and useless churning of gears in my mind create some space for patience and perspective, and maybe even a little joy.

Dave was a godsend.

Layers of Acceptance

And so here I sit, in the middle of my one and only life. With support and friendship, with love felt so fiercely it radiates all through me. I sit with the intense beauty of that love, made stronger because I am acutely aware of it. Aware of the gift that right now, in this very moment, I am here.

I also feel the fragility of time. Fear and sadness sit beside me as well. Like the lower ranked wolves in a pack, they are always looking to take over the dominant position. They wait, they watch, and they look for any crack in the shell. Any small sliver, and they quickly wedge themselves there, vying for the top spot in my days.

This delicate space between the two extremes was not entirely foreign. My first rodeo provided unwanted experience in these opposing grabs of fear, and love and gratitude. Amidst it, life went on. The question was how to live it. How to create a mindset that processes all the chaos into an existence that feels right. One that finds a way to tolerate, compartmentalize, or transform the threats to happiness into something manageable, something to make life worth living.

Back then, I relied on the data to get through. All my decisions were made based on facts, objectively. Feelings were relevant, but they didn't hold credibility like the real meat and potatoes in the numbers. Numbers don't lie, even if we don't like them or wish them to be different. In the case of a tie, stick to the numbers.

I researched my condition, the mechanics of it, various treatments, and their efficacy. Most of that research is tied to survival numbers, an asymptotic curve that shows the likely duration of survival under various treatment scenarios. After my first round of treatments, I was 90 percent likely to survive five years. A 90 percent chance that I'd make it to the other side and walk on with this behind me. In the world of cancer, 90 percent is a really great number. The science made me well physically. Therefore, it made me well mentally. With a number like 90, I was comforted enough to make cancer smaller, only faintly present. When I had doubts that I'd end up in that 10 percent bin, I thought of all the new developments in cancer treatment. I'd be fine.

This second round of cancer, an advanced cancer, has sharper edges and lots more grit. What do you do when your number falls to zero, no *done with treatments!* No living end point to look forward to and celebrate? Even worse, what do you do when your worldview, one committed to the institution of science, has nothing to get you past zero?

My mental stability shattered. All possible intensities were in play, and every decision had severe consequences. Right at my life's peak of decision making, the pillars of my reasoning—stick to the science—crumbled. I sat in a pile of hard sooty rubble, confused at the broken foundation around me, thinking *How could you leave me now?*

Stripped of all irrelevancies, this apex of our core beliefs is engrained in the deepest of values. The individual, innate beliefs entrenched in our bones. Data wasn't going to bring any comfort, yet a quick switch to a different foundation seemed impossible. So, I stuck to the science, but shifted to the outliers. Those unexplainable datapoints that aren't tightly grouped with all the others. Sure, that survival curve heads towards zero, but there were a few Stage IV cancer fighters that found a way out. Why? How? If I could just figure out how they persisted, maybe I'd make it through. But outliers are harder to decipher than datapoints that group neatly. I flailed with them.

I kept searching with every bit of my cancer's progression. I spent hours in tormented research of unconventional alternatives, weighing side effects, drug efficacy, and timelines that shocked me every time I saw them, numbers that couldn't possibly relate to me, until I landed on a new course of treatment. With each switch, there was the hope that this med would work, that it would at least exceed my estimated time of effectiveness and stretch time like soft taffy. But simply put, my cancer was aggressive. Each med I took only lasted half as long as the expected average, but I still held on to the hope that next med would work better.

This was my future, one hard to find comfort in. I couldn't think myself into a place of peace, and I couldn't escape Stage IV. It seems it takes something big enough and insistent enough, like our own mortality, to force us to re-evaluate the things that we hold most dear. The values that guided how I carved my way through life no longer fit. It was uncomfortable, to challenge my ideology, without at least a pause in cancering. When we're willing to accept that there might be something more, or, even harder, something different, that's when real growth happens. With a small, well-placed shift in the way we view the world and our place in it, maybe we can find something more in our existing selves.

Much of this work, to find peace in living with advanced cancer, was internal, solitary work. But this was much too big for me alone. I needed something more, something different to help me find a way to live my one and only life. I saw myself standing with cancer alone, even with a wide cast of support. They were desperate to carry this load for me. The love they give was an enormous support. But as much as they propped me up, there was still a slight chasm among us. The lives of the healthy versus the one on a different course. At my lower points, the space between us felt wider.

I felt so very alone after a bad scan one day. I needed a connection but didn't have the energy to seek it out. About a year earlier, Autumn sent me a blog link from a previous co-worker who also had stage IV breast cancer. She offered it as a source of understanding that only those with the disease could provide. For about a year, I left the blog link untouched. But that day I gave it a try. In the first post I read, someone told the blogger, "If anyone can beat this, you can."

A statement that grossly simplified the disease and placed the burden of survival on the afflicted. It also inferred cancer could readily be outwitted, defeated with will, as long as we put in the effort. The blogger readily dismissed this line of thinking, noting how insulting it was to those whose will to live was just as strong. Cancer is just mean. Sometimes unstoppable.

I found comfort in this, simply because it was a truth. Not from the facts and figures of science, but a truth of empathy and compassion. There was a gentleness that I found so sooth-ing. That we can do absolutely everything right, but still get overpowered by a disease we don't fully understand. We should all take it easy on ourselves. Science provides amazing insights into cancer, and I'm still counting on it to find new treatments before I reach the end of the known suite. But that's for survival, not for *living*. I needed to build a new foundation, one rooted in humanity. I needed a new destination, one where a long life wasn't the only success. I looked for more connections to help me find it.

I listened to a podcast by Kate Bowler, an "author, tod-dler-wrangler, and professor at Duke Divinity School" who also has stage IV cancer. She talked with a friend and pediatric oncologist about his experience working through cancer with families and patients. He relived a life-changing experience with one patient he lost, an experience that temporarily broke him. I was resistant to listening to it, because I had been avoiding the emotional parts of cancer. They horrified me. But since the science couldn't help me on how to live well, I needed to try something else. After everyone else in my family went to bed, I sat at my kitchen table and listened.

Kate and her guest talked about how, for some cancers, the focus is entirely getting to the other side, to remission or cure. Her guest compared the various treatment options to vines and helped me visualize swinging from vine to vine to get to the other side. I found this totally relatable and consistent with my experience so far. I was grasping each vine fiercely until it was ready to give way, then I'd reach for the next one. I focused on those vines with sharp intensity. Every one of them. I took stock of how many were left, how far each will travel, all the while calculating if they will take me far enough. To further hedge my bets, I tried weaving new vines from shreds of alternative medicine as I was riding. I was putting the true value of living and all my focus on making it to the other side.

It didn't change my number from zero. All that obsession on the vines and the other side was consuming me. It was removing my peripheral vision. Worse yet, desperation pushed the pace of time even faster, defying the odds was the only win. Energy taken from living a whole life in the present.

Yet this - this day, this moment, this second—this was all I would get. Right now, I still got to ride. I needed to figure out what it meant to ride well. Setting terminal illness to the side meant letting go of control. It meant letting go of my hawk-like attention to the vines allow view of all the other colors in a fully embraced life. I decided to step into my own experience.

Which means talking about dying.

Kate and her guest talked about how sad it was when someone died. They talked about how hard and how kind it can be to let people go. They talked about how to be with someone when there are no words. They talked about these things in detail. I was astounded that they said these words out loud. I nearly exploded right there at the table. I sobbed. I cried for the people they had lost, for their own grief, for myself. And at the end I felt - relieved. I took a few deep breaths to settle myself and said right out loud: *I am going to die.*

Emotional acuity is made in slow gains, like wading through molasses. Yet it's also a seesaw of revelations that calm and realities that terrify. There is a fine line between hope and desperation. Hope allowing us to live in joy, to feel good in the moment and let go of all the scary thoughts of what ifs. Hope allows us to think of the future, at least the near future, without fear. To think of our present as a path to good things. But working so hard to convince ourselves that our hope is solid can turn it to a starving need draped in panic. It is a tough place to be when a bad scan comes in, harder to recover from when you're far on the desperation side of hope.

On the other end of the spectrum, there is an equally fine line between realism and cynicism, a combination that sits on top of a high cliff, only a few steps away from the long fall into despair. I am wary of that cliff; afraid it's a one-way trip. I stay far from it. Instead, I stay between the lanes of hope and pragmatism. The overcorrection to get back in the safe lanes is sharp and jarring. It throws me out of control. Too far out into wishing for all the time in the world, only to come crashing down with a bad scan that reminds me I won't get it.

It is an exhausting, relentless road, cancer is.

Recently, during another transition in medicines, I wondered how this new med would assault me. I walked through a couple weeks both silent and desperately needing to talk. I was starting to veer more broadly on the outside of the hope and realism bounds that define "okay" for me. I was unable to stop thinking about the consequences of cancer, the dark side of realism. I was getting pulled strongly towards despair.

I needed connection but didn't have the energy to pick up the phone. I sat in my car deciding who to call. My sister and I talk almost daily. She meets me in any mental state and doesn't hesitate to lay herself down to absorb as much of my sorrow as she can. She's done that over and over. And over. And over. I'm sure she is drained from it, but she'll do it again every time anyway.

I could call my mom. My mom provides support that is limitless. But we're so similar it's almost too raw. I felt her worry at the slightest difference in the tone of her voice, the pause between sentences, an exhale only a fraction of a second longer than normal, the tempo of her words. All of her fears and emotion transferred through a main line right into me. It's like an overload of electricity that travels both ways. It's too much.

Jon was always there. But I get so annoyed at being the one who brought this to us. The repetition of him sating my needs only reminds me of how perpetually needy I am. It makes me so angry that I don't want to ask for more in that familiar seat again.

I needed someone familiar with that throbbing pull of hard times who knows what it's like to oscillate between the bounds of "okay." It's hard to find a person who can relate to the wear of great strife at all when you're in your late thirties to early forties. I don't really fit in the décor of mountain bikes and kayaks. Because I'm the first one of my peer group to go through a life-threatening illness, I am like a fancy piece of cut glass. I get the attention of everyone I'm around. They're fascinated by me, by the foreign ways I throw light around the room. But I'm something to handle carefully, so as not to break me, which really just makes you afraid to get near me at all.

I sent a message to Tammy, my old college roommate. She's had her own roller coaster in the past few years, with intense highs and lows. There's something about experiencing those highs and lows that removes the need to describe how much they suck. I needed someone who could relate. Tammy could. I sent her a text.

Hi Tam.
Hey M, tell me something good.

It took me off guard. I was ready to talk about what was happening. "I had a scan yesterday." Or "I'm changing meds" or blah-blah-blah cancer. But something good? I didn't have anything good to talk about. And I had been so focused on the work and scheduling and drag of it all, I hadn't noticed anything—not one other thing—around me. It took me a while to come up with something.

Caitlin smiled this
morning. Warmed
my heart. Tell me
something good...

I didn't leave
anything at home today
(I usually do)

I get to watch Lily
dance tonight

Awesome! I have my
dance classes tonight

Tammy worked as a social worker in Philadelphia. It was a career change she found later in her career. It was a calling that allowed her to bring all of her personal experience with mental illness and the huge challenges that come with it into helping families in need. She sets aside time to plan around hard things during her first meeting with the families she works with - from how to keep a child from cutting themselves, to how to keep a family from losing their home. She opens up these meetings with "celebrations." What is going well? They all come up with something to celebrate. Big or small. Sometimes she hears things like, "I made it through the day."

Sometimes making it through the day is the best we can do. I find that when I'm having a bad day it starts to feel like I'm sliding down the inescapable cliff into despair. I keep thinking that if I can get better at dealing, I'll be able to avoid those bad days. But then Jon reminds me, "Sometimes you're going to have bad days, and that's okay."

This was my challenge. To calmly look cancer's ugly in the eye and stare it down as it made itself comfortable. And then to also see the big, colorful, rich rest of my life beyond it, even though cancer has plopped itself down right in the middle of all that is mine.

That asshole.

I will keep trying new treatments, and I'll tolerate all their side effects. I'll research my options every time there is a bad scan and decide what's next. I haven't given up, but I have moderated my expectations. I still hope that some miracle of medical advancement will prolong my life beyond what the numbers say. But that's not the only thing I hope for.

My hope is to be myself in spite of it.

To not let isolation take over by reaching out to people and saying really scary things.

To accept what is, the good and the bad, without being consumed by the dark sides.

To be thankful, because I'm able to see some good fortune.

To be happy, because there still are things to be happy about.

To not let cancer take me, before it takes me.

These are my hopes.

Now that I've accepted that I probably won't make it to the other side, my job was to help everyone around me with the transition. To do it as well as we can. My greatest hope is that after I'm gone all of the people around me will have no regrets. The thought of anyone I love having regrets absolutely horrifies me.

I'd been trying so hard to shelter the girls from all of this. To hide the details and spare them the worry. To make it so that they can just be teenagers and not steal their childhood under the shroud of, "My mom is sick." But I realized that in shoving cancer under the rug, I've been denying them the chance to process it with me. By avoiding the all the really hard conversations—AT ALL COSTS—I've only been pushing them off to someone else. And I'm the mom. And right now, I'm here.

I have no words for this though. I have no idea what to say or how much to say. This is an impossible conversation. One that I knew I had to have. So, one night after another bad scan, I came home, sat down on the couch and said, "Girls, we have to talk."

Lily and Caitlin.
Caitlin and Lily.

"Being deeply loved by someone gives you strength,
while loving someone deeply gives you courage."

— Lao Tzu

"I love to see a young girl go out and grab the world
by the lapels. Life's a bitch. You've got to go out and
kick ass."

— Maya Angelou

O ver the past months, years, I tried to keep the girls
around the edges of my cancer; I'd worked to avoid
making the topic taboo. That worked well. *I have cancer and so I do all these weird things* became normal. But I didn't
get into the heavier stuff, the frightening stuff. Instead, we only

skimmed the surface when talking about cancer and my treatments. I thought that I was being strong around them, to shelter them, to never show my vulnerabilities, doubts, and fears. The last true update I gave them was months ago, when there was a mixture of good and bad news. I emphasized only the good parts, of course, and tried to say it casually so that it wouldn't hurt too bad.

I told them that my treatments had knocked back nearly all of the cancer except that one stubborn spot that was resistant to treatments. I didn't tell them that the resistance was bad. Resistance meant progression and loss of time. I told them that there was one spot left, and the doctors were going to radiate it away. I didn't say that it was kind of an experiment. That we'd have to wait and see if that worked. And I didn't tell them that we didn't know if there were other resistant spots at well.

"Wait, Mom. So, you only have one spot left? And they're going to get rid of it? You'll be cancer free!"

I saw their joy and felt the hope and relief that washed over them like a wave. I knew that I should set the record straight and also knew what an undertow that would be. I was speechless, literally completely unable to make a sound. Because you have to breathe to make a sound, and it knocked the wind right out of me, grabbed hold of my innards in a death grip. The moment passed before I could get up for air, and they bounded out of the room. I let them be misguided.

I only needed three radiation treatments to zap that stubborn spot. Not knowing how I'd fair in the treatments, I told them of the schedule and that we'd have to just wait and see how it went.

We didn't talk about radiation during the week of treatments. Life went on as usual. Until the last day, a Friday. Jon and

I sat having coffee together that morning before the girls got up, as we always do. At one point he asked me, "So what are you doing today?" I stared at him for a moment, deciding whether I should attack him or not. *You forgot what's happening today? Are you freaking kidding me?* Instead, I looked at him deadpan, with very direct eye contact and said, "I'm getting a final treatment to blast a hole into my liver today. What are you doing?"

But Lily didn't forget. My daughter who wasn't all that fond of extended affection. She rarely tells me how she's feeling; but when she does, I'd stop everything to listen, because it was a rare gift. She practically ran into the house after school and fell into me fiercely, squeezing tightly, and whispered, "You're cancer free Mom. Cancer free." I hugged her back trying not to cry, feeling treasonous for being so shy of honest, but unable to ruin the moment she poured into that tight hug.

But my daughters ongoing questions let me know the things that gnawed at them. Caitlin saw through my unintentional deception, because she takes time to really see people. She paid such close attention to me, to my actions, and moods.

"So, Mom, why do you still take so many pills if they got rid of that last spot?" My attempt at honesty was to say that it could always come back. That I'd never be out of the weeds or free of dealing with this. I hadn't had the scan yet that indicated that wasn't the only resistant spot. But it was still many steps shy of the truth.

And when the next round of meds made me horribly nauseas and flu-like for months, "Why are you taking a medicine that makes you so sick? Aren't these medicines supposed to make you better?" I didn't tell her that I tolerated the horrible side effects because the alternative was worse. I didn't talk about the alternative. I just said we're trying to get a handle on the side effects.

They both knew that something was still wrong, and when they questioned me to make sense of it, I gave them non-answers. But I couldn't find the words.

But it was time. Maybe in part because I'd finally come to realize that I couldn't get out of this. Acceptance didn't come in one all-encompassing revelation. It trickled in as small bits of realized truths. My mortality took a while to fully dawn on me. Sheltering the girls would just postpone what they would have to face, leaving someone else to grieve with them.

I started reaching out to others to help find a way to do this. I talked with Autumn, and she gave such good advice: that big news can be best delivered in small doses. The first thing I had to make clear was that the cancer wasn't gone and really never would be. I talked with another friend who had lost his wife to cancer when their son was the same age as the girls. We walked slowly along the shoreline of Lake Superior while he relived their experience to tell me how his wife confronted her diagnosis with her son. Through his own pain, he told me how she talked to her son about how much strength it would take to face her illness, her mortality. I was completely blown away and starting to see what I needed to do.

So, on a day after another bad scan, I decided it was time. Jon and I drove home from the cancer center in quiet. We stopped at home briefly, but the girls didn't feel like going out to eat, so Jon and I went out without them. Even though we didn't talk about cancer over dinner, or the upcoming conversation about cancer, it was an emotional break. The respite I needed between the intensity of my appointment at the cancer center that day and what was going to be a gut-wrenching conversation with the girls.

Jon and I sat in silence on the way home from the restaurant. We pulled into the garage and sat in the car, neither of us wanting to walk into what was next.

"So, are we going to talk to the girls?" he asked softly.

"Yep, let's do this. This is going to be fun." I started to open the car door abruptly. "Yeah, looking forward to this."

"Hold on," he reached out and laid a hand on my leg to keep me from running. "Do you want to sit down for a sec?" I closed the door. We waited in silence for another moment. "Do you know how you want to do this?"

"I have no idea." I rubbed my eyebrows in concentration and also to shelter myself from the rising panic in my chest.

More silence. More waiting.

Jon spoke slowly, cautiously. "Maybe we can say something like this. 'Mom has stage IV cancer. Stage IV means there is no cure. It is in her, and probably always will be." He was speaking with such deliberate gentleness that I almost lost my nerve. "Treatments work to slow it down, but at some point, this kind of cancer will likely advance."

He stopped to look at me. I took my hand from my eyebrows and kept staring at the floor. He took a breath and kept going. "For a while there, the treatments knocked it back, but the doctor said today that it has spread. Stage IV means spread."

Jon has such a calming way of stating things simply and completely, without judgement or conjecture beyond what needs to be said right now. He makes big ugly things less difficult to look at, less scary. He said the necessary words that hurt my heart, helping me find the guts to say them myself. I had to say these things. I hated them. But they were mine to say.

And I said them. We called the girls in to our family room and sat on our fluffy, U-shaped couch. The couch that was big enough for all of us to lie down when we watched movies on Friday nights, sharing blankets when it was cold. The couch that could seat a few more when we played games with friends. The very same couch that I sat on often to let one of the girls lie across my lap, so I could tickle their face with a small shred of paper or play with their hair.

I repeated what Jon said practically verbatim. Each word stabbing me in the heart. I watched my daughters receive those words. I don't remember if I cried as I said them. I might have squeaked out a tear, but I didn't fall apart. I looked them in the eye and saw that they understood what I was telling them. They fully got it. If they resented me for misleading them over the past six months, they didn't show it at all. I wouldn't have blamed them for being angry. At me, at the situation, at everything and nothing. But I didn't see anger. I just saw the deep sorrow of understanding.

I can't say that things changed drastically after that. They didn't pull away, and they didn't cling closer. We were as close as we've always been, maybe a little tighter. We kept on going, living our lives as well as we could. We all have days that are hard, and we each navigate them in our own way, in the ways we reach out or need to pull away a bit. I pay closer attention to where they are and try to throw up soft bumpers to keep them in the lanes of okay. I have no idea if I'm doing it well. But I'm trying like hell and doing the best I can.

I do know that I am most okay when I'm around Jon and the girls. When I'm away from them, anxiety sits in my chest without exception. Because when I'm not around them I feel absent.

There was no stage of enlightenment in cancer for me. I didn't have a sense of peace. I didn't have some zen-ed out acceptance of any of it. I viciously despised it. And I was so very sorry that the life my girls should have, one that takes their mom for granted until they are at least 30 years old, was robbed of them by this disease. I struggle, nearly every day, to not be consumed by that, so that my girls can know a mom of love, and not one of bitterness and rage.

I told them, later, when the cancer spread to my spine, to my ribs, and let them know that they could ask me anything, anything at all. I kept bringing it up occasionally, just to keep the door open for when they're ready to talk. I saw them deflate every time in a way that said *Please don't bring that up, Mom.* But I have to.

I talked to them about strength. Knowing that we're all more introverted, I told them it's okay to grieve on your own, but it is essential that we come together as a family in hard times. I've tried to prevent them from isolating themselves from each other when I'm gone, whenever that may be, because moms have a special kind of glue in a family. Jon assures me that he won't let them drift away. I make him promise regularly. It's as far as I can get when imagining what their lives will be like without me, how this will change them all.

My parenting changed with this new acceptance of things. I focused more on building confidence and less on getting them to clean their rooms. (As a result, their rooms are utterly disgusting. I can't even go in there. This may not be the best approach. Eh. Oh well.)

I tell them I love them constantly. I don't leave a day, or the room, or a conversation without saying it. And they return it every time. I tell them in as many ways as I can what strong young women they are, because they will need that to bounce back. They'll be devasted, and that stab of grief might not ever fully go away, but they will bounce back. They'll know that I'm in them, in all the ways they remember me, in the inherited traits I've passed on, and in the mannerisms they've picked up from me without realizing it. I'll live on as a part of them. And that can never be taken away.

I find a small solace in gratitude for making it as long as I have. When I see them play volleyball and roar at each other with excitement, or when they've crushed a hit or dug out a hard pass, I think *I am just so freaking happy to be here. That I got to see this. That I made it this far.* When they tell me some new revelation in knowing themselves and the world around them, I feel what a gift it is to know that change in them. I avoid like hell thinking of the revelations I will miss. I focus on the moment, this moment, wrapped in the warmth that, for just today, I got to understand them just a little bit more. I see them glance at each other with a shared understanding when I embarrass them. (They're teenagers. I embarrass them regularly.) It makes me thankful for the tight bond they share, a bond I've seen strengthen even more in the last few years. It will help them support each other throughout their lives in a way that only sisters can.

I don't know how our conversations will change as things progress. I leave space for enough hope that another vine will come down for me, and I won't miss as much as I thought I would. My new focus, and singular purpose, is to find and figure out every possible way to make the steps to my death as complete and gentle as they can be.

I'm no longer running from death. I've stepped fully into my reality and started staring death in the eye, only enough so that I'm ready when Mihailo has to tell me that there are no more treatments for me. He dreads it as much as I do, and it will be awful. Someone has to tell me all these horrible things, and I am eternally grateful that Mihailo does it with such care and empathy. I'm equally thankful that I'll only have to live through that news once, while he'll have to deliver it again and again.

I remember listening to a radio show years ago, before I ever had cancer, about a training for oncology staff. They brought together nurses to talk through patient care in the face of terminal illness. All of them were asked, *If you could choose, how would you choose to die?* They talked through the options. Not by murder, too violent. Not by tragic accident, too abrupt. Think of all the unsaid things? One by one they considered each end. And they all came to land on death by cancer. Why? Because you have time to plan, time to think through the things that need to be said, and time to share those things with the people you love.

It goes without saying that there was some lack of creativity or serious editing in that radio show. Dying of old age in your sleep is clearly the best choice, if given it. (Duh.) I still don't choose cancer. I would never. I thank cancer for nothing. But if I end up having to go far too early, I can front load telling my girls how much I love them and how enormously proud I am to be their mother, over and over, to make up for the years they won't hear me say it.

You two are the very best of everything I've ever known. I could not love you more.

Winter

They've been dancing for so long. Keeping it up amongst the fatigue, their hatred of it, the blisters on their feet. The music begins to slow, and then fade. When it stops completely, they stand still, staring at each other.

It's only when they turn back from the edge of the rooftop that they see them all, scattered around the dance floor. The woman right beside them had been there, guarding the edge in the path of her twirl. She smiled to let them know she was ready; she's been ready to catch them the whole time. There's the man who put the chair out for them, just to make things a little bit easier. There's the one who kept them in bounds with a touch so soft they never realized till now. There's the one who put her own life on hold, looking, searching, finding things to help. It was this crew who picked the best music, who set down the soft floor. Some had been on the roof the entire time; others came running as soon as they heard her cry.

They hadn't seen all these people during Tango. They were so focused on the dance, the dance. Focused on every move, on every effort. They concentrated so fiercely on each hand position, each footfall, each turn of the head, each possibility of a new song to dance to. They didn't look down. Dear God, don't look down. Don't get distracted from this dance. The Tango is everything.

The Tango is not everything.

The dancers see it now. See the bonds of love that connect them all. The harsh abrasive glow of the moon is outdone by the bright colors that swirl around them now. The colors of love. Together, they fill the roof with more than Tango. They laugh, and cry, and hug, and love each other fiercely. They will hold nothing back.

They have danced all the Tango they can; there is no more Tango left. They have tried every version of this dance to escape it, but the moon would not relent. It is time for this dance to end. They are ready. They stay as close as possible as they leave irrelevancies here, making more room to soak up the true marrow of their lives. Surrounded by their people, he sits on the chair to take off those horrible fucking shoes. God, he has hated these shoes. He sets them under the chair and then looks to find her. She is standing in front of him with her hands on her hips. She's been waiting, watching him, right then seeing him even more clearly. With his shoes placed under the chair, he stands up to her. She grins at him, slowly caresses his cheek and kicks off her shoes under the chair as well.

It is time to leave the rooftop. Together, they walk over to the door with the frosted glass. The metal hinges whine as they pull it open, the rooftop's final swan song. Surrounded by their people, they cross the threshold of the frosted door and walk off the roof for the last time.

Acknowledgments

This book would not have come to completion without the help of so many people. To everyone who showed me support and encouraged me along the way, I sincerely thank you.

Thanks to my early readers who gave me such good feedback and even more so encouraged me to keep going. Heidi Colton, Tammi Etris, Bob Rice, Michael Mozdy, Sandy Raimondo, Sharon Frazey, Jon Wheeler, Heather Ferry, my Mom Marilyn McCarthy.

Thanks to my first editor, Rachel Stout, who encouraged me to really "go there" and let the full experience of my story shine through. Thanks to Jen Lalich who pushed me to have the courage to show the beauty and the harshness of my life through the book. And thanks to Parker Sterling who helped me find my voice during the writing process and pushed me to always bring my best work to every page.

Thanks to the publishing team at Bublish. You helped me through the process at every step. From cover and interior design, to developing and implementing a marketing strategy.

Most of all, thank you to my family for your support on the days when I thought I'd never complete this thing. Thank you for believing in me.

And thanks to the super fine Mr. Jon Wheeler for coming up with the best title ever.

CPSIA information can be obtained
at www.ICGtesting.com
Printed in the USA
LVHW110739120820
662962LV00004B/1199